汉语位移动词语义中的方式/结果互补性研究　江苏省高校哲学社会科学一般项目
（项目号：2018SJA1586）

汉语位移动词中的方式结果互补性研究

——共时与历时视角

The Manner/Result Complementarity in Chinese Motion Verbs:
Synchronic and Diachronic Perspectives

邱磊　著

浙江工商大学出版社
ZHEJIANG GONGSHANG UNIVERSITY PRESS
·杭州·

图书在版编目(CIP)数据

汉语位移动词中的方式结果互补性研究:共时与历时视角 / 邱磊著. —杭州:浙江工商大学出版社，2022.11

ISBN 978-7-5178-5180-6

Ⅰ. ①汉… Ⅱ. ①邱… Ⅲ. ①汉语—动词—研究 Ⅳ. ①H146.2

中国版本图书馆 CIP 数据核字(2022)第206496号

汉语位移动词中的方式结果互补性研究
——共时与历时视角

HANYU WEIYI DONGCI ZHONG DE FANGSHI JIEGUO HUBUXING YANJIU
——GONGSHI YU LISHI SHIJIAO

邱磊 著

策划编辑	姚 媛
责任编辑	张莉娅
责任校对	林莉燕
封面设计	朱嘉怡
责任印制	包建辉
出版发行	浙江工商大学出版社
	(杭州市教工路198号　邮政编码310012)
	(E-mail:zjgsupress@163.com)
	(网址:http://www.zjgsupress.com)
	电话:0571-88904980,88831806(传真)
排　版	杭州朝曦图文设计有限公司
印　刷	杭州宏雅印刷有限公司
开　本	710mm×1000mm　1/16
印　张	13
字　数	234千
版印次	2022年11月第1版　2022年11月第1次印刷
书　号	ISBN 978-7-5178-5180-6
定　价	65.00元

Abbreviations

ADV	Manner adverb marker 地 de (Li, Thompson, 1981)
ASSO	Associative meaning of 的 de (Li, Thompson, 1981)
ASP	Aspect marker
BA	Disposal construction with 把 bǎ
BEI	Passive construction with 被 bèi
CONJ	Conjunction
CL	Classifier
CRS	Current relevant situation
DUR	Imperfective durative aspectual marker 着 zhe
NEG	Negative
NEG.POT	Negative potential marker
NOM	Nominalizing particle 的 de (Li, Thompson, 1981)
PART	Particle
POSS	Possessive marker
POT	Potential marker
PROG	Progressive

Contents

Chapter 1 Introduction ·· 001

  1.1 Research Questions and Significance of This Study ·············· 003

  1.2 The Typology of Motion Events and Motion Verbs ·············· 009

  1.3 Lexicalization Patterns of Motion Events in Chinese ············ 012

  1.4 Structure of This Study ·· 015

Chapter 2 Previous Studies and the MRC Hypothesis ·············· 019

  2.1 Lexicalist Approaches to the Lexicon and Syntax Interface············· 021

  2.2 The MRC as a Lexical Constraint ······························ 028

      2.2.1 The Motivation for the MRC: Integration of Verb Roots and Event
             Schemas ·· 028

      2.2.2 Semantic Notions Underlying Manner and Result Verbs ········ 028

      2.2.3 Hallmarks of Manner and Result Verbs ···················· 032

      2.2.4 Disentangling Various Manners and Results ················ 034

  2.3 Arguments Against the MRC Hypothesis ······················ 036

      2.3.1 Arguments Based on Counterexample Verbs in English ········ 037

      2.3.2 Arguments Against the MRC as a Constraint Operating in the
             Lexicon ·· 044

  2.4 Summary ·· 051

Chapter 3 The Manner/Result Complementarity in Modern Chinese

·· 053

3.1 Previous Studies of Classification of Modern Chinese Motion Verbs ··· 055

3.2 Notions of Manner and Result in Chinese Motion Events ·············· 062

3.3 Re-examination of the Lexicalization Patterns of Chinese Motion Verbs ··· 065

    3.3.1 A Preliminary Distinction ······································· 065

    3.3.2 Controversies over Classification of Some Motion Verbs ········ 071

    3.3.3 Potential Counterexample Verbs ···························· 075

    3.3.4 Neglected Motion Verbs in Previous Studies ···················· 079

3.4 Summary ·· 093

Chapter 4 The Manner/Result Complementarity in Old Chinese ··· 095

4.1 Background of Old Chinese ··· 099

    4.1.1 Key Typological Characteristics of Old Chinese ··············· 099

    4.1.2 Motion Events in Old Chinese ···························· 104

4.2 Research Method and Data ··· 105

4.3 Lexicalization Patterns of Motion Verbs in Old Chinese ············· 109

    4.3.1 Preliminary Classification of Motion Verbs in Old Chinese ······ 109

    4.3.2 Purported Counterexamples to the MRC in Old Chinese ········ 112

4.4 Summary ·· 127

Chapter 5 The Diachronic Evolution of Polysemous Motion Verbs ··· 129

5.1 The Evolution of Motion Verbs in Their Lexical Semantics and Grammatical Behaviors ·· 132

    5.1.1 走 zǒu "walk/run" ······································· 133

    5.1.2 飞 fēi "fly" ··· 137

    5.1.3 跑 pǎo "run" ··· 139

5.2 Factors Affecting the Change of the Lexicalization Patterns of Motion Verbs ··· 141

    5.2.1 Possible Factors Affecting the Evolution of the Lexicalization

Patterns of 走 zǒu "walk/run" ······················ 141

5.2.2 Extending the Analysis of 飞 fēi "fly" and 跑 pǎo "run" ········ 161

5.2.3 The Lexical Evolution of Polysemous Motion Verbs as an Epitome of the Evolution of Chinese Motion Lexicon ················ 166

5.3 Summary ·· 169

Chapter 6 Conclusion ·· 171

6.1 Summary of Major Findings of the Present Study ················· 173

6.2 Motion Verbs and Motion Constructions at the Lexicon and Syntax Interface ·· 177

6.2.1 Polysemous Manner-of-Motion Verbs in Cross-Linguistic Contexts ··· 177

6.2.2 Lexical Semantics and Morphosyntactic Structure ··············· 179

6.2.3 Diachronic Change of the Lexicalization Patterns of Motion Verbs ··· 180

6.3 Future Work·· 181

References ·· 185

List of Tables and Figures

Table 1 Periodization of Chinese Language ·······················015

Table 2 Hallmarks of Manner and Result Verbs ·······················034

Table 3 Word Pairs Involving Derivation via Tone Alternation ···············101

Table 4 The Evolution of the Grammatical Behaviors of 走 zǒu "run" from Old to Middle Chinese ·······················135

Table 5 The Use of 走 zǒu "run/walk" in Source-Oriented Path Sense in Premodern Chinese Period ·······················136

Table 6 The Frequency of Occurrence of V+去 qù "go" and V+走 zǒu "walk" as V2 in Causative Motion Events in Modern Chinese ·······················158

Figure 1 The Evolution Processes of 走 zǒu "run/walk", 跑 pǎo "run" and 飞 fēi "fly" ·······················140

Figure 2 The Factors Affecting the Lexical Evolution of 走 zǒu "run/walk" ······160

Figure 3 The Factors Affecting the Lexical Evolution of 飞 fēi "fly" ···············165

Figure 4 The Factors Affecting the Lexical Evolution of 跑 pǎo "run" ············166

Chapter ❶

Introduction

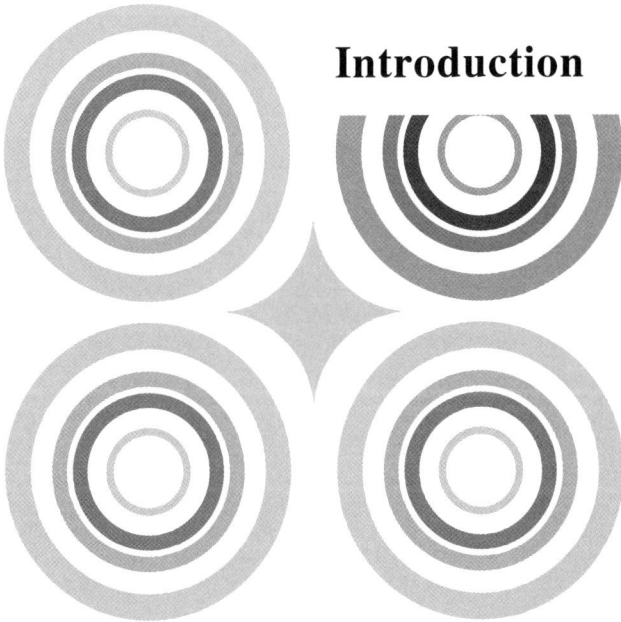

1.1 Research Questions and Significance of This Study

In the last few decades, in the study of the interface between the lexicon and syntax, the role of construction has been increasingly appealed to in explaining argument realization patterns and syntactic distribution of verbs, whether in generative (Hoekstra, Mulder, 1990; Ramchand, 2008; Acedo-Matellán, 2010; Harley, 2005) or cognitive linguistic approach (Goldberg, 1995, 2010; Goldberg, Jackendoff, 2004). In this vein, the meaning of verbal roots may be built with no constraint on its complexity, and in particular the role of a verb is only to provide a coherent semantic frame that evokes "a generalized, possibly complex states or events that constitute a cultural unit" (Goldberg, 2010). Thus, the lexical semantics of verbs has been largely reduced to be trivial in explaining their relevant grammatical behaviors. However, the question is whether there is indeed no constraint on the complexity of verbal meaning. Contrary to the theoretical position of taking lexical meaning as a complex without constraint and trivial to grammatical behaviors of verbs, I will argue in this book that verbal meaning may be constrained in a systematic way, and lexical semantics is important to determine and constrain the grammatical behaviors of verbal predicates. In particular, I will look at a systematic lexicalization gap in verbal meaning proposed by Rappapport Hovav and Levin (1998, 2010) and Levin and Rappaport Hovav (2013) that manner and result meaning components lexicalized in verbs are in complementary distribution. A verb may not lexicalize both at a time. They dub it the manner/result complementarity (MRC).

(1) Manner/result complementarity: Manner and result meaning components are in complementary distribution: a verb may lexicalize only one.

(Levin, Rappaport Hovav, 2013)

According to this hypothesis, verbs which specify the way of carrying out an action cannot encode what result the action brings about, and in contrast, verbs which express something acquire a state that may not elaborate in what manner the state is acquired. Example verbs of each type are provided by Rappaport Hovav and Levin (2010) as in (2).

(2) Manner verbs: nibble, rub, scribble, sweep, flutter, laugh, run, swim, etc.

Result verbs: clean, cover, empty, fill, freeze, kill, melt, open, arrive, die, enter, etc.

The MRC is obviously reflected by the contrastive lexical entailments from pairs of verbs in change of state domain such as scrub and clean. While the manner verb scrub requires the agent to perform an action in a particular way without requiring any resultant state to come about, the result verb clean encodes the resultant state the theme acquires without specifying any particular action by the agent, as exemplified by sentences in (3).

(3) a. Mary scrubbed the bathtub, but it is still dirty.

b. Mary cleaned the bathtub by scrubbing it/wiping it.

The MRC is observed not only in change of state domain, but also in motion domain. Parallel to verbs in change of state domain, motion verbs also demonstrate comparable complementarity of meaning components, as motion in specific direction is also regarded as a type of result related to the spatial property of an entity. Manner-of-motion verbs such as walk and run only describe the manner in which the motion is carried out and leave direction of motion unspecified. Path verbs such as enter and arrive express motion in particular direction with reference to a landmark but leave the manner unspecified.

Though the MRC hypothesis is implicit in various approaches to lexicalization patterns (e.g. Talmy, 1985, 2000; Bevears et al., 2010), it has also been challenged by a number of scholars, such as Goldberg (2010), Mateu and Acedo-Matellán (2012), etc., who name a number of counterexamples which are claimed to encode both manner and result. Cross-linguistic studies of the viability of the MRC based on languages such as Polish, Greek, etc., (Bialy, 2013) have also been explored. In spite of empirical evidence gained in previous studies for the MRC, there is still no consensus upon the status of the MRC.

The classification of motion verbs as manner and path verbs in Talmy's (1985, 2000) typology of motion events is consistent with the MRC hypothesis, but in the study of motion events, manner-of-motion verbs across languages also seem to show varied grammatical behaviors. They demonstrate complex aspectual properties cross-linguistically and their classification and analysis are often controversial, raising interesting and challenging issues for lexical semantics (Kubota, 2014). The encoding of motion events in Chinese and the classification of Chinese motion verbs are also subjected to much controversy. As to the typology of motion events encoding, scholars (Zlatev, Yangklang, 2004) have claimed that besides the prototypical manner and path verbs which are dominantly used in satellite-framed languages and verb-framed languages respectively, there exists the third type of verbs encoding both manner and path in serial verb languages which are often classified as equipollently-framed languages such as Thai and Chinese. If true, this type of verbs would undermine the validity of the MRC. In addition, though some motion verbs are regarded as either prototypical manner or result verbs in Chinese, their grammatical behaviors seem to contradict the properties of relevant type of verbs. For example, in Modern Chinese, when the basic motion verbs 滚 gǔn "roll" and 跑 pǎo "run", both unanimously regarded as manner verbs by scholars, are used in succession, the direction of the motion "departure from a reference object" is entailed. As illustrated in (4), the rubber ball's departure from the original place is entailed in the meaning of the verbal compound 滚跑 gǔn pǎo "roll-run", since the cancellation of this direction of motion results in ungrammaticality of the sentence.

(4) 皮球　　　滚　跑　了，*但　　它　还　在　原地①。

    píqiú　　　gǔn　pǎo　le　dàn　tā　hái　zài　yuándì

    rubber.ball　**roll**　**run**　ASP　but　it　still　at　　original.place

    "The rubber ball rolled away, #but it is still at the original place."

The questions are where the direction of motion comes from and whether these manner verbs also lexicalize the direction of motion thus constituting counterexamples to the MRC. Both the lexicalized meaning components and grammatical behaviors of these verbs need to be clarified.

In addition, scholars (Ma, 2008; Shi, Wu, 2014) observe that in Old Chinese, a typologically distinct language from Modern Chinese with respect to motion events encoding, there is a group of manner verbs, which also encode the goal direction of motion, as they can be directly followed by reference objects to indicate the goal of motion. As seen in (5), the verb 奔 bēn "rush" is directly followed by the reference object 燕 yān "the State of Yan". Then does the MRC hold for a typologically different language like Old Chinese?

(5) 王子　　　克　奔　燕。(《史记》)

    wángzǐ　kè　bēn　Yān

    Prince　　Kè　**rush**　**Yan.State**

    "Prince Ke rushed to the State of Yan."

Furthermore, though some motion verbs in Modern Chinese have evolved from

---

① Throughout the book, the Chinese example sentences are represented in four lines. In the first line the sentence is given in simplified Chinese characters, which are followed by Pinyin, the official Romanization system of Chinese characters in the second line. The gloss and the literal translation of the sentences are given in the third and fourth line respectively. * stands for ungrammaticality of the target sentence in question and # stands for ungrammaticality of the literal translation in English.

their ancestors rooted in Old Chinese, both their ontological categorization as manner or result verbs and their relevant grammatical behaviors have changed. For example, while the verb 走 zǒu "run" in Old Chinese can be followed by reference ground to indicate the goal of motion as in (6)a, it cannot be used in this way in Modern Chinese in (6)b. What factors have contributed to its evolution in ontological categorization and grammatical behaviors?

(6) a. 百濮　　离　　　　居, 将　　　各　走　其　邑。(《左传》)
　　　Bǎipú lí　 jū jiāng   gè zǒu qí yì
　　　Baipu scattered live will   each **run his town**
　　　"People of Baipu live in scattered communities and they would go back to their own town".
　 b. *走/跑　　学校
　　　zǒu/pǎo   xuéxiào
　　　walk/run   school
　　　"walk/run to school" (Intended meaning)

These questions are all related to the ultimate viability of the MRC as a lexical principle constraining the complexity of verbal meaning on the one hand and the property of the lexicalization patterns of Chinese motion verbs on the other hand. This book aims to clear up some of the aforementioned problems and questions surrounding the MRC hypothesis and examine its cross-linguistic viability based on Chinese motion constructions. Generally, this book tries to answer the following questions.

i. Do the lexicalized meaning components in Modern and Old Chinese motion verbs conform to the MRC hypothesis?

ii. Concerning their lexical semantics and grammatical behaviors, what evolutionary processes have motion verbs undergone along with the development of the Chinese language from Old to Modern Chinese?

iii. What factors affect the ontological categorization and grammatical behaviors of Chinese motion verbs?

iv. From a diachronic perspective, what is the possible relation between lexical semantics of Chinese motion verbs and the syntactic structures they may appear in?

To answer these questions, I set out with an exploration of motion verbs in Modern Chinese. With regard to the controversy over the classification of Chinese motion verbs, based on the main tenets of the MRC, I use a set of consistent criteria to classify motion verbs in Modern Chinese into either manner or result verbs. Focusing on the counterexample verbs in Modern Chinese proposed by scholars, I also explore their lexicalized meaning and grammatical behaviors so as to clarify their ontological status. The evidence in Modern Chinese shows that purported counterexamples in Modern Chinese pose no real challenge to the MRC, as these counterexamples either actually lexicalize only one type of meaning components and derive the other from the contexts or are polysemous motion verbs encoding only one meaning component in one use but not the two together. The evidence in Old Chinese show that though it is a typologically distinct language, it also conforms to the MRC. The case studies of the evolution processes of three motion verbs 走 zǒu "run/walk", 跑 pǎo "run" and 飞 fēi "fly" indicate that the ontological categorization of verbs as manner or result and their relevant grammatical behaviors may be affected by both conceptual components of verbs and morphosyntactic structures in the language. As important meaning components encoded in verbs, the notions of manner and result reflect the two-way interaction between semantics and syntax.

The significance of this study is threefold. First, it will promote a better understanding of possible constraints on verbal meaning complexity and how a verb contributes to the encoding of motion events. The synchronic comparison and contrast between verbs incorporating different conceptual information and the analysis of the diachronic evolution of motion verbs with the similar conceptual components will help to uncover the nature of verbal meaning and to see whether the lexicalized verbal meaning is constrained by certain lexical principle and represented with semantic structure independent of syntax. Second, it will further reveal the property of lexicalization patterns of Chinese motion verbs. As a serial verb language with very limited morphological devices to mark the grammatical status of words, the lexicalization pattern of Chinese motion verbs is subjected to controversy. The synchronic and diachronic study of the lexical semantics and grammatical behaviors of Chinese motion verbs will further illuminate the possible conceptual components packed in Chinese motion verbs and how they affect verbs' grammatical behaviors. Third, it can enhance a better understanding of the nature of the interface between semantics and syntax in motion domain. The conceptualization of motion events and their relevant linguistic representations provide an ideal research field to reveal how the verbal semantics interact with syntactic constructions. On the one hand, motion events tend to include similar conceptual components such as manner and path of motion, but on the other hand these conceptual components may be represented with different syntactic elements. Motion verbs with variable grammatical behaviors within and across languages are in particular intriguing to study. A closer look at the Chinese motion verbs and constructions will shed light on a better understanding of the interaction between verbal meaning and the syntactic structure.

1.2 The Typology of Motion Events and Motion Verbs

Motion is central to human's activity and the encoding of motion events reflects the relation between thought and language. Talmy (2000) describes a motion event as a situation containing movement or maintenance of a location. To express motion events, languages tend to include similar conceptual components. Talmy (2000) develops an analysis of transitional motion events with four basic conceptual components, as illustrated in (7).

(7) Figure: the moving entity

Ground: the entity that the Figure moves in relation to

Motion: the presence of motion

Path: the course followed by the Figure with respect to the Ground

These conceptual components may be packed in a sentence to express a single motion event. For example, in (8), the sentence describes the Figure (Phil) carried out a Motion (move) along the Path (towards) with respect to a Ground (the window).

(8) Phil   moved   towards   the window.

Figure   Motion   Path   Ground

Besides the main event composed of the four components, co-events expressing the manner or cause of motion may also be included in motion events encoding. For instance, in (9), besides the figure's motion into the cave, the verb run also specifies the manner in which the motion is carried out.

(9) He ran into the cave.

Though languages tend to include similar conceptual components to express similar events, they show systematic distinction as to how these conceptual components distribute across constituents in a sentence. Based on Talmy's motion events typology, languages which incorporate path into the main verb are called verb-framed languages with languages such as Spanish, French, Korean and Japanese falling into this type; in contrast, languages which incorporate manner into the main verb but encode path as satellites are called satellite-framed languages with English, Russian and German as representative languages. The distinction between two types of languages can be attested in a pair of sentences expressing the same scene in English and French in (10). In (10)a the manner of motion is incorporated into the verb fly, but in (10)b the path is encoded in the verb sort "exit".

(10) a. An owl flew out of the hole in the tree. (Slobin, 2004)

     b. D'un trou de l'arbre sort un hibou.

of.a hole of the.tree exits an owl

"An owl came out of a hole in the tree." (Slobin, 2004)

(Cited in Levin & Rappaport Hovav, 2014)

In addition, serial verb languages such as Thai, Emai, and Ewe are found to encode both manner and path into verbs, so a third type of language is suggested, i.e. equipollently-framed languages (Slobin, 2004; Zlatev, Yangklang, 2004). For example, in (11) manner and path are both expressed in main verbs in Thai.

(11) chán dəən khâw paj

I walk enter go

"I am walking in (away from the deictic center, into something)."

(Zlatev, Yangklang, 2004)

However, recent work argues that the two fold or three fold classification of languages appears to be too simplistic, as languages often use more than one type of lexicalization patterns to express motion events. It is argued that most languages use both verb-framed and satellite-framed lexicalization patterns, and some languages are even attested to use all of the three patterns.

Besides the differences reflected in language structures, the typological difference can also be attested from the size of the motion verb lexicon. Based on a series of studies, Slobin (2004) finds that satellite-framed languages tend to have a larger manner verb lexicon. Similarly, Verkerk (2014) also finds the correlation between the language type and the size of the path verb lexicon: Verb-framed languages tend to have a larger path lexicon.

In addition, motion verbs from typologically different languages are also reported to have distinct lexicalization properties. Slobin (2004) and Shi and Wu (2015) point out that verb-framed languages are more likely to accept a kind of semantically synthetic verbs in which both manner and path are encoded simultaneously. In equipollently-framed languages such as Thai, used in serial verb constructions between pure manner and pure path verbs, a type of motion verbs

汉语位移动词中的方式结果互补性研究——共时与历时视角

| | | | | | | | | | | | The Manner/Result Complementarity in Chinese Motion Verbs: Synchronic and Diachronic Perspectives

such as tók "fall", lòn "fall", lóm "collapse", hòklóm "trip and fall" and com "sink" are also said to encode both manner and path information. For instance, phlòo "pop out" expresses a motion going through a landmark and also some manner-related information such as purposive action. (Zlatev, Yangklang, 2004) Though the lexicalization patterns of these verbs have not been talked about under the rubric of the MRC, if they indeed lexicalize the two components together, they challenge the validity of the MRC.

1.3 Lexicalization Patterns of Motion Events in Chinese

As a serial verb language, Chinese may use more than one motion morpheme to encode motion events. However, as there is no overt morphological marker to indicate the grammatical status of the co-occurring verbal morphemes, there is an everlasting debate concerning the typological status of Chinese among researchers. Talmy (2000, 2009) considers Chinese as a satellite-framed language. His evidence for this position is that when more than one verbal morpheme is used in motion event constructions, the manner verb is the main verb of the sentence, and the path verb is used as a subordinate complement to the manner verb, because usually pronounced in neutral tone and with reduced argument structure the path morpheme does not behave like a full-fledged verb. For example, in (12) the manner verb 走 zǒu "walk" is regarded as the main verb of the sentence and the path verb 出 chū "exit" is believed to be a complement of the manner verb. Researchers such as Peyraube (2006), Ma (2008) and Lamarre (2008) also embrace Talmy's position.

(12) 她　走　出　了　病房。
　　 tā zǒu chū le bìngfáng
　　 She **walk exit** ASP hospital room
　　 "She walked out of the sickroom."

Contrary to the Talmy's position to regard Chinese as a satellite-framed language, Tai (2003) identifies Chinese as a verb-framed language, because he believes that path verbs are actually the predicate center of the multi-morpheme motion constructions. His evidence for this position is that it is the path verb but not the manner verb that can be attached with aspectual marker -le. As he illustrates in (13), the verb 过 guò "cross" incorporating path is the center of the verb compound 飞过 fēi guò "fly cross", since it can be used alone with aspectual marker -le to indicate the completion of passing the channel as in (13)b.

(13) a. 约翰　　飞　过　英吉利　海峡。
　　　　Yuēhàn　**fēi**　**guò**　Yīngjílì　Hǎixiá
　　　　John　　**fly**　**cross**　English　Channel
　　　　"John flew across the English Channel."

　　 b. 约翰　　过　了　英吉利　海峡。
　　　　Yuēhàn　**guò**　**le**　Yīngjílì　Hǎixiá
　　　　John　　**cross**　**ASP**　English　Channel
　　　　"John crossed the English Channel."

　　 c. *约翰　　飞　了　英吉利　海峡。
　　　　Yuēhàn　**fēi**　**le**　Yīngjílì　Hǎixiá
　　　　John　　**fly**　**ASP**　English　Channel
　　　　"#John flew the English Channel."

(Tai, 2003)

An obvious problem with Tai's analysis is that he does not make distinction between the semantic and syntactic center of the Chinese verbal compound 飞过 fēiguò "fly across". Talmy (1985, 2000, 2009) suggests that, path is always the core schema of a motion event, but whether a language is a satellite-framed or verb-framed is determined by what syntactic element the core schema is realized. If a language is regarded as verb-framed, it should render the path into the main verb of the sentence. Since the verb 过 guò "across" expresses the path of the motion, it is normal that it represents the semantic center of the predicate, but its status as the semantic center of the predicate does not ensure its status as the main verb of the sentence. In fact, it is the verb 飞 fēi "fly" rather than 过 guò "across" that should be considered as the main verb of the sentence and thus Tai's argument of classifying Chinese as a verb-framed language is problematic.

Based on another line of research, i.e. the pragmatic preference for certain conceptual components (e.g. path, manner, and ground) exhibited in language use, Chen and Guo (2009) argue that Chinese is actually an equipollently-framed language, because the number of types of manner verbs used in Chinese lies between satellite-framed languages such as English and verb-framed languages such as Spanish. In addition, based on their statistical analysis of motion expressions used by Chinese native speakers, they demonstrate that Chinese native speakers use path verbs and manner verbs to the same degree. Thus they conclude that based on the Chinese patterns of expressing motion events it is neither a satellite-framed nor a verb-framed but an equipollently-framed language. Nonetheless, to determine the typological status of a language based on only pragmatic preference in language use is not reliable, as the unique morphosyntactic structures available in a specific language may make the statistics based on language use not completely comparable.

Some researchers (e.g. Shi, Wu, 2014) point out that things are not as simple as they appear to be. Languages may use varied patterns to encode motion events and thus show typological features of all three types. Moreover, questions such as why languages tend to have varied motion event expressions and where the different lexicalization patterns come from naturally arise. From a diachronic perspective, Shi and Wu (2014, 2015) investigate the historical evolution of Chinese lexicalization patterns of motion events and find that from Old to Modern Chinese period, Chinese has undergone radical changes in its morphosyntactic structures and correspondingly its patterns of motion event expressions have also evolved from verb-framed to satellite-framed type. Their argument is supported by their analysis of language structures and language use of Chinese in four historical periods. As to language structures, though serial verb constructions formed as $V1_{manner}$-$V2_{path}$ are acceptable in both Old and Modern Chinese, their grammatical status has evolved from double-head pattern to single-head pattern, which indicates that though in Old

Chinese path verbs are also the head of motion constructions, in Modern Chinese they have involved into satellites subordinating to manner verbs. As to language use, the verbal constructions depicting motion events in Old Chinese mostly encode path information (74.53%), but in Modern Chinese they mostly encode manner and path by V1s the main verb and V2s the satellites respectively (70.39%). (Shi, Wu, 2014) This shows that Old Chinese should belong to the family of verb-framed languages and Modern Chinese belong to the family of satellite-framed languages.

I continue this study under the assumption that though Modern Chinese language dominantly encodes motion events into satellite-framed patterns, it uses various ways to encode motion events, and more importantly it has undergone a typological shift from verb-framed to satellite-framed language since Old Chinese period.

The periodization of Chinese language in this study is adopted from Sun (1996), as given in Table 1.

Table 1　Periodization of Chinese Language

Period	Date
Old Chinese	500 BC–AD 200
Middle Chinese	AD 200–1000
Pre-modern Chinese	1000–1900
Modern Chinese	1900–present

It should be noted out that the periodization of Chinese language has not been universally agreed upon. The reason that I follow Sun's periodization is that the division into the four periods is mainly based on the syntactic development of the Chinese language. Relatively different syntactic properties of Chinese in each period provide good reference for the evolution of motion verbs and constructions.

1.4　Structure of This Study

Following this introduction, which briefly presents the background of the research including main tenets of the MRC, research questions, and motion constructions and motion verbs in Chinese, the remainder of this book is organized as follows.

In Chapter 2, based on a review of lexicalist approaches to the lexicon and syntax interface, I will introduce the theoretical motivation of the manner/result complementarity hypothesis. The semantic notions underlying the two types of verbs will also be illustrated in detail. Arguments against the MRC based on counterexample verbs in English and different views of the linguistic phenomena related to the MRC hypothesis will be discussed.

Chapter 3 checks the validity of the MRC with respect to the lexicalization patterns of motion verbs in Modern Chinese. I start with a review of previous studies on the classification of Modern Chinese motion verbs paying particular attention to the controversial verbs which are classified differently by previous researchers. To get a comprehensive understanding of the lexicalization patterns of Modern Chinese motion verbs, I also reanalyze the sample motion verbs collected by Chen and Guo (2009) from nine novels clarifying their ontological category. Three basic motion verbs 走 zǒu "run/walk", 跑 pǎo "run" and 飞 fēi "fly", which exhibit inconsistent grammatical behaviors but are neglected by previous researchers are looked at in detail. The result shows that these verbs are actually polysemous motion verbs with separate manner and result senses thus conforming to the MRC hypothesis.

Chapter 4 investigates the lexicalization patterns of motion verbs in Old Chinese. As Old Chinese is said to be typologically distinct from Modern Chinese, key typological properties, research methods and relevant data of Old Chinese are firstly explained. With reference to sample verbs collected by Ma (2008), a preliminary classification of Old Chinese motion verbs is conducted and it shows that motion verbs in Old Chinese can also be divided into manner and result verbs conforming to Rappaport Hovav and Levin's (2010) proposal. Lexical meaning and grammatical behaviors of purported counterexample verbs are analyzed and it is demonstrated that these potential counterexamples do not violate the MRC encoding actually only one meaning component at a time.

Focusing on polysemous motion verbs with varied grammatical behaviors in Modern and Old Chinese, Chapter 5 delves into an investigation into the diachronic evolution of their lexical semantics and grammatical behaviors. Possible factors affecting their distinct way of ontological categorization and grammatical behaviors are analyzed. The result indicates that the lexicalization patterns of these motion verbs result from varied factors related to pragmatic inference, cognitive preference, change of morphosyntactic structures and grammaticalization. The ontological categorization of motion verbs may be affected by not only conceptual components encoded in verbs but also the available morphosyntactic structures of the language.

Chapter 6 concludes the whole study. Synchronically, studies on both Modern and Old Chinese show the lexicalization patterns of Chinese motion verbs conform to the MRC. However, diachronically the ontological categorization of verbs may be affected by not only conceptual components of verbs but also the morphosyntactic structures of the language. As important meaning components are encoded in verbs, the notions of manner and result reflect the two-way interaction between semantics and syntax.

Chapter 2

Previous Studies and the MRC Hypothesis

Based on a review of lexicalist approaches to the lexicon and syntax interface, this chapter explicates the theoretical framework related to the MRC so as to clear theoretical and empirical grounds for further studies in the Chinese language. The theoretical motivation for the MRC, the semantic notions underlying the two types of verbs and the hallmarks of manner and result verbs will be illustrated. Arguments against the MRC based on counterexample verbs in English are discussed and show that the purported counterexamples do not challenge the validity of the MRC. Two approaches which observe the linguistic phenomena corresponding to the MRC but deny its status as a lexical constraint are also reviewed to indicate that the MRC cannot be understood as deriving from different syntactic configurations or differences in aspectual focus. Rather it is a viable principle operating in the lexicon.

2.1 Lexicalist Approaches to the Lexicon and Syntax Interface

The MRC hypothesis has its roots in the theoretical orientation that the behavior of a verb, particularly its argument realization patterns, is largely determined by its meaning. Generative semanticists make efforts to find structured lexical representation of verb meaning in various forms which are intended to capture those meaning components determining verbs' grammatical behaviors, as an alternative to the generative syntactic approach, which takes the grammatical behaviors of verbs to be derived from syntactic configuration. This line of work starts with the introduction of thematic grid in the lexical entries by Stowell (1981), who proposes that the thematic grid determines the syntactic structure a verb may

汉语位移动词中的方式结果互补性研究——共时与历时视角

| | | | | | | | | | | | The Manner/Result Complementarity in Chinese Motion Verbs: Synchronic and Diachronic Perspectives

appear in. Though the general theoretical assumption underlying the idea of the thematic grid that the lexical-semantics specified in the lexicon is projected into syntax is still endorsed by Levin and Rappaport Hovav (1995) and Rappaport Hovav and Levin (1998, 2010), this early form of projectionist theories obviously has its drawbacks. For example, the thematic grid fails to capture and explain the fact that the same verb may appear with more than one set of morphosyntactic realization options for its arguments. In addition, lexical representation as the thematic grid also suffers problems. For instance, there is no consensus about which and how many roles are needed, the lack of internal organization, etc. (Rappaport Hovav, Levin, 2010)

Predicate decomposition approaches which assume "verb meanings can be decomposed into basic components" (Levin, Rappaport Hovav, 2005) take up the endeavor of isolating and representing the recurring meaning components which determine the range of argument alternations that a verb can participate in. Jackendoff (1987) puts forward lexical conceptual structures, which consist of primitive conceptual categories such as Thing, Event, State, Action, Place, and Path. There are some rules that can be used to expand these basic categories into more complex expressions, as in (14). For example, Jackendoff explains that combined with a Thing argument as a spatial reference point, the basic category Place can be expanded into a Place-Function which defines a region in (14)a.

(14) a. PLACE [$_{Place}$ PLACE-FUNCTION (THING)]

b. PATH [$_{Path}$ TO/FROM/TOWARD (THING/PLACE)]

c. STATE [$_{State}$ BE/ORIENT (THING, (PATH/PLACE)]

(Jackendoff, 1987)

With these primitive categories, lexical entries with argument structure such as into and run can be represented as in (15).

(15) a. $\begin{pmatrix} \text{into} \\ [-N, -V] \\ [\underline{\quad} NPj] \\ [_{Path} \text{ TO } ([_{Place} \text{ IN } ([_{Thing} \quad]j)])] \end{pmatrix}$

    b. $\begin{pmatrix} \text{run} \\ [-N, +V] \\ [\underline{\quad} (PPj)] \\ [_{Event} \text{ GO } ([_{Thing} \quad]i, [_{Path} \quad]j)] \end{pmatrix}$

(Jackendoff, 1987)

More importantly, the co-indexes between the conceptual structure and the subcategorization in lexical entries ensure the elements in conceptual structure that are mapped into syntactic structure correctly. For example, the conceptual structure of the sentence "John ran into the room." in (16)a can be represented as (16)b. The indexes indicate that the first complement of the conceptual category GO is mapped as the subject, and the complement of the conceptual category IN is realized as the noun in the prepositional phrase.

    (16) a. John ran into the room.

        b. $[_{Event} \text{ GO } ([_{Thing} \text{ JOHN}]), [_{Path} \text{ TO } ([_{Place} \text{ IN } ([_{Thing} \text{ ROOM}])])])]$

(Jackendoff, 1987)

However, in Jackendoff's framework, all conceptual components encoded in verbs, linguistic and nonlinguistic, are treated with equal status, so the distinction between meaning components which have grammatical consequences and those that do not is blurred. On the one hand, this leads to undergeneralization of verbs sharing the same structural meaning. For example, verbs such as run and drink both denote activity by an agent, but the common property shared by them is lost in their lexical conceptual structures, as can be seen from (15)b and (17).

$$(17) \begin{bmatrix} \text{Drink} \\ \text{[-N, +V]} \\ \text{[\_\_\_ (NPj)]} \\ \text{[}_{\text{Event}}\text{ CAUSE ([}_{\text{Thing}}\text{]i, [}_{\text{Event}}\text{ GO ([}_{\text{Thing}}\text{ LIQUID]j)]} \\ \text{[}_{\text{Path}}\text{ TO ([}_{\text{Place}}\text{ IN ([}_{\text{Thing}}\text{ MOUTH OF ([}_{\text{Thing}}\text{]i)])])]} \end{bmatrix}$$

(Jackendoff, 1987)

On the other hand, as there is no clear criterion for determining the number and type of primitive conceptual categories, it is not clear why some notions but not others should be used as basic categories to delineate word meaning. For example, as noted by Fan (2013) it is not clear why MOUTH should be used as a basic category for the verb drink, but not LEG for run. What's more, Jackendoff (1990) later includes a significantly greater number of basic predicates, which makes his theory face the same problems as theories of semantic roles. How to identify a small, comprehensive, universal and well-motivated set of predicates is the key to the problem (Levin, Rappaport Hovav, 2011).

The predicate decomposition approach adopted by Levin and Rappaport Hovav (1995) and Rappaport Hovav and Levin (1998, 2001) makes distinction between structural and idiosyncratic meaning encoded in verbs. Only a small set of the information related to linguistic representation is included in their structured lexical representation. The lexical decomposition of a verb is made up of both aspects of meaning. While the idiosyncratic part is encoded in terms of constants, the structural part is encoded in terms of a small set of lexical-semantic templates formed via various combinations of basic event predicates such as ACT, CAUSE, and BECOME, and constants such as STATE, MANNER, THING, PLACE, and INSTRUMEN. Because lexical-semantic representations formed as such correspond roughly to Vendler-Dowty aspectual classes of verbs, they are often called "event structure templates". The basic inventory of event-structure templates is listed in (18).

(18) Lexical-Semantic Templates

a. [x ACT <MANNER>] (activity)

b. [x <STATE>] (state)

c. [BECOME [x <STATE>]] (achievement)

d. [[x ACT <MANNER>] CAUSE [BECOME [y <STATE>]]]
   (accomplishment)

e. [x CAUSE [BECOME [y <STATE>]]] (accomplishment)

(Rappaport Hovav, Levin, 1998)

Rappaport Hovav and Levin further explain that though the set of event-structure templates is fixed, the set of constants is open-ended. Each constant has an ontological type which determines its basic association with a particular event-template and these associations are formulated via "canonical realization rules". The basic canonical realization rules are given in (19).

(19) Canonical Realization Rules

　　a. manner ⟶ [x ACT <MANNER>]

　　b. instrument ⟶ [x ACT <INSTRUMENT>]

　　c. placeable object ⟶ [x CAUSE [BECOME [y WITH <
　　　THING>]]]

　　d. place ⟶ [x CAUSE [BECOME [y <PLACE>]]]

　　e. internally caused state ⟶ [x <STATE>]

　　f. externally caused state ⟶ [[x ACT] CAUSE [BECOME [y <
　　　STATE>]]]

(Rappaport Hovav, Levin, 1998)

As illustrated by the canonical realization rules in (19) there are two ways constants are associated with event-structure templates. They can either be modifiers of predicates as in (19)a and (19)b or arguments of predicates as in (19)c–(19)f. In addition, the position that a constant can be inserted into must be consistent with its ontological type. For example, as in (19)b an "instrument" constant can only be inserted into the modifier position of an event structure denoting activity to modify the primitive predicate ACT. Similarly, the constant categorized as "externally caused state" can only be inserted into event structures denoting accomplishment or achievement as argument of the primitive predicate BECOME as in (19)f.

Besides representing the basic meaning of a verb, much of the variation in verb meaning may also be achieved by the process called Template Augmentation Rule suggested by Rappaport Hovav and Levin (1998).

(20) Template Augmentation Rule

Event-structure templates may be freely augmented up to other possible templates in the basic inventory of event-structure templates.

Taking the verb sweep as an example, used in its basic meaning it is associated with the lexical semantic template denoting activity in (21)b. In (21)c the lexical semantic template is augmented to that of (21)d by combining the activity-denoting template with externally caused change of the state template.

(21) a. Terry swept the floor.

b. [x ACT <SWEEP> y]

c. Terry swept the floor clean.

d. [[x ACT <SWEEP> y] CAUSE [BECOME [y <CLEAN>]]]

To ensure that the arguments in lexical semantic templates project into the syntactic structures accurately, Rappaport Hovav and Levin (1998) also propose a series of well-formedness conditions and linking rules on the syntactic realization of lexical-event structures. There are two well-formedness conditions, namely, Subevent Identification Condition and Argument Realization Condition.

(22) a. Subevent Identification Condition:

Each subevent in the event structure must be identified by a lexical head (e.g. a V, an A, or a P) in the syntax.

b. Argument Realization Condition:

b1. There must be an argument XP in the syntax for each

structure participant in the event structure.

b2. Each argument XP in the syntax must be associated with an identified subevent in the event structure.

(Rappaport Hovav, Levin, 1998)

Rappaport Hovav and Levin's approach to account for the grammatical behaviors of verbs has advantages over previous theories of thematic roles or lexical conceptual structures. It avoids the proliferation of unlimited arbitrary thematic roles or basic conceptual categories by putting forward a limited set of lexical semantic templates. On the one hand, thematic roles are no longer unrestricted roles associated with arguments related to every single use of a verb; rather they are abstracted labels that occupy certain positions of a well-motivated and limited set of lexical semantic templates. On the other hand, the meaning components encoded in verbs are distinguished between those linguistically represented and those not. The proposal of this independent level of predicate decomposition not only enables the encoding of predicates' lexical meaning but also induces restriction on the possible types of meaning. As Beaver and Koontz-Garboden (2012) note, according to Rappaport Hovav and Levin's event-structure typology, only an individual or an action but not the change of state can be a causer argument of a primitive predicate CAUSE. Beaver and Koontz-Garboden (2012) further illustrate that as there is no event structure like (23), no verb can possibly encode the meaning such as "x dying caused y to die".

(23) [[x BECOME <dead>] CAUSE [y BECOME <dead>]]

The idea of MRC hypothesis is also proposed to follow from the properties of event structures and is implicit in Rappaport Hovav and Levin's (1991, 1995) early work, but it is explicitly proposed based on the association between verb roots and event structures. The specific theoretical motivation for the hypothesis will be explained in the next section.

2.2 The MRC as a Lexical Constraint

2.2.1 The Motivation for the MRC: Integration of Verb Roots and Event Schemas

Rappaport Hovav and Levin (2010) suggest that the complementarity distribution exhibited by pairs of manner and result verbs like swipe and clean is not merely a statistical tendency, but rather it derives from the way verb roots are associated with event schemas. As mentioned in the previous section, manner and result roots belong to different ontological types and thus have distinct positions in event schemas: a manner root can only be a modifier of the primitive predicate ACT and a result root is the argument of the primitive predicate BECOME, as in (24)a and (24)b. It is also proposed that a root has only one position in an event structure. Thus it is predicted that there will be no single verb involving an event structure associated with two distinct positions ruling out the formulations like (24)c and (24)d and then leads to the emergence of two natural classes of verbs: manner and result verbs.

(24) a. [x ACT<MANNER>]

b. [[x ACT] CAUSE [y BECOME <RESULT>]]

c. [[x ACT <ROOT1>] CAUSE [y BECOME <ROOT2>]]

d. [[x ACT <ROOT>] CAUSE [y BECOME <ROOT>]]

2.2.2 Semantic Notions Underlying Manner and Result Verbs

The classification of verbs into the manner or result type is also supported by independent semantic notions underlying the two types of verbs: Manner and result verbs are associated with non-scalar and scalar changes respectively in their lexical semantics. Drawing from studies of scale structure in lexical semantics (Kennedy, 2001; Kennedy, McNally, 2005), Rappaport Hovav and Levin (2010) propose a scale is "a set of degrees—point or intervals indicating measurement values—on a particular dimension (e. g. height, temperature, cost), with an associated ordering relation". A scalar change in an entity involves a change in the value of one of its scalar-valued attributes in a particular direction. They also emphasize that though all dynamic verbs involve change, result verbs differ from manner verbs fundamentally in involving scalar changes, as they lexically specify a scale which represents an attribute of their argument and a change in value of this attribute in a particular direction along the scale. For instance, as explained by Rappaport Hovav and Levin (2010) the verb warm describes a change associated with a scale on the dimension of temperature, and the scale is made up of values in an increasing order, so the argument it predicates undergoes a measurable change from a lower temperature to a higher one and thus it is regarded as scalar changes. In contrast, manner verbs lexicalize non-scalar changes which are complex and cannot be characterized by an ordered set of values of a single attribute. For example, the verb jog, also illustrated by Rappaport Hovav and Levin, involves a specific sequence and pattern of movements of legs, though different from the action of walk, collectively these movements do not represent a change in the value of a single attribute and thus cannot be measured by a scale, so it involves non-scalar changes.

Result verbs can be further divided into subtypes according to what kind of scales they are associated with. Verbs such as break and crack involve changes associated with two-point scales, which only have two values characterized as either having or not having a particular property. Since the transition from one value to the other is conceptualized as instantaneous, this subtype of result verbs is a true achievement, showing aspectual property as punctual and telic, as illustrated in (25).

(25) a. The egg cracked in a minute/*for a minute.

b. The child broke the vase in a minute/*for a minute.

Verbs such as increase and decrease involve changes associated with multi-point scales, which have many values concerning certain property of an entity. Rappaport Hovav and Levin note that change of state verbs associated with multiple-point scales are often called "degree achievement" or "gradual change" verbs. This subtype of result verbs can be interpreted as telic or atelic aspectually, as in (26).

(26) Her temperature decreased in/for 10 minutes.

Parallel to change of state verbs, in motion domain it is also possible to classify motion verbs as involving scalar and non-scalar changes with manner-of-motion and directed motion/path verbs[1] encoding non-scalar and scalar changes respectively. According to Rappaport Hovav and Levin (2010), in motion events a scale is about a spatial relation or the dimension of distance. It can be understood as a set of contiguous points of location ordered in the direction of movement between the theme and the reference object forming a path. Scalar and non-scalar verbs in motion domain can be differentiated by checking whether they involve changes specifying such a scale. Manner-of-motion verbs do not specify the spatial relation or distance between the theme and reference object, and thus involve non-scalar changes. In contrast, directed motion verbs can be characterized with respect to a scale. As Rappaport Hovav and Levin explain, the location of the theme on the path represents a value for its distance with respect to a reference object. Along with the directed motion, the location of the theme changes, which can be characterized as change in the value of the scale and thus can be understood as involving a scalar change. They illustrate this with the verb ascend: Ascend lexicalizes a scale on the dimension of spatial distance, and the points in its scale are ordered against the direction gravity. If a figure ascends, the value on the scale necessarily increases.

In addition, according to Rappaport Hovav and Levin (2010), result verbs from two domains also show parallel telicity patterns depending on whether they involve a two-point or multi-point scale. Directed motion verbs involving two-point scales such as enter and arrive are punctual and telic. Directed motion verbs involving multi-point scales such as ascend and descend can be interpreted as telic or atelic, though they are different from manner-of-motion verbs in that they can gain telic reading without supporting context (Rappaport Hovav, Levin, 2014). Crucially, the varied aspectual features demonstrated by result verbs associated with different scales can be detected by checking their grammatical behaviors when used with

---

① In this book, the terms "path verb" and "directed motion verb" are used interchangeably.

different types of time adverbials.

However, result verbs from the two domains also show variations as to how the scale they are associated with is expressed. While ordered scales involving a property of an entity are inherently valued and in most cases fully specified in verbs, scales related to spatial relation may not be inherently ordered, but are determined with respect to a reference object. For example, the change of state verb cool necessarily involves an entity showing a decrease in the value of the attribute of temperature, so as a result of the cooling event the value of the temperature must be lower than the original one. Contrastively, directed motion verbs such as exit, enter and return only lexicalize part of the path information and the exact direction of motion can only be determined with respect to a reference object, which is usually specified as ground information and realized as complement of the motion verb or just contextually implied. Nevertheless, as argued by Rappaport Hovav and Levin (2010) there are indeed a few verbs including ascend, descend, fall and rise which fully lexicalize the direction of motion with reference to the pull of gravity.

As to scalar changes, a special distinction based on whether the scale is specified in the lexical entry needs to be made. Rappaport Hovav and Levin (2014) argue that a scale can be compositionally formed from a lexical head in combination with its arguments and adjuncts to represent the aspectual feature of a predication, but result verbs involving scalar changes are only restricted to those verbs which fully or partially specify a scale in their lexical meaning with the only change of state and directed motion verbs falling into this type. Another type of verbs, namely incremental theme verbs such as eat, read, wipe, etc., though also involve a scale with regard to extent or volume of the theme, should not be grouped as result verbs, as they do not lexically specify an attribute that a scalar change is based on and show distinct grammatical behaviors and argument realization patterns from result verbs. For instance, though the aspectual feature of result verbs can be completely predicted from what kind of scales (two-point vs. multi-point; bounded vs. unbounded) they are associated with, the aspectual feature of incremental theme verbs can only be regarded as a compositional feature related to both the verb, the theme and adjunct of the predicate. In other words, an incremental theme verb itself cannot determine the aspectual feature of the predicate.

2.2.3 Hallmarks of Manner and Result Verbs

The way that manner and result verb roots are associated with event schema and the independent semantic notions two types of verbs involve can be detected syntactically by examining their argument realization patterns and aspectual features. For example, manner verbs involve a simple event structure with only one structural argument, i. e. the agent of the action, whereas result verbs involving a complex event structure with two structural arguments, i. e. the arguments of CAUSE and BECOME. According to the argument realization rules illustrated in previous Section 2.1, i. e. "there must be an argument XP in the syntax for each structure participant in the event structure", it follows that manner verbs but not result verbs allow unspecified or unsubcategorized objects as illustrated in (27) and (28).

(27) a. Leslie swept (the floor).

b. He reads himself quasi-blind.

c. 30 dairy cows ate themselves to death.

(28) a. *Kelly broke again tonight when she did the dishes.

b. *The clumsy child broke the beauty out of the vase.

While in (27)a the manner verb sweep allows its normal object "the floor" to be unspecified, and in (27)b read and in (27)c eat allow unsubcategorized objects, the result verb break in (28) does not allow unspecified and unsubcategorized objects, since the patient arguments are the structural argument of the primitive predicate BECOME and thus must be realized syntactically.

The semantic notions of scalar and non-scalar changes underlying result and manner verbs also make them exhibit distinct grammatical behaviors. Manner verbs do not encode changes which can be measured in terms of any single scale, so it's easy to form the second predicate by adding various scale-denoting XPs to manner verbs. The example in (29) shows the motion verb run is compatible with phrases expressing different path information "out of the store" or "into the store", as run itself does not encode any path information.

(29) John ran into/out of the store.

In addition, as manner verbs involve complex immeasurable non-scalar changes, they are generally atelic. As can be seen in (30), manner-of-motion verbs roll and run are only compatible with durative time adverbial "for X time".

(30) a. The ball rolled for two minutes/*in two minutes.

b. Avery ran for an hour/*in an hour.

In contrast, scalar changes encoded in result verbs make them very restrictive in combination with scale-denoting XPs in that only scale-denoting XPs which are compatible with or further elaborate the lexicalized scales in result verbs can be added. The examples in (31) show that the verb arrive is compatible with the location phrase "at the station" which further elaborates the path information expressed by the verb, but it is incompatible with the adjective "tired", as it involves another scale different from the one expressed by the verb.

(31) a. Mary arrived at the station.

b. *Mary arrived tired. (With intended meaning: Mary became

tired as a result of her arrival.)

Furthermore, result verbs associated with two-point scales are necessarily punctual and telic. The examples in (32) show arrive and crack are telic and not compatible with durative time adverbial "for X time". When used with a frame time adverbial "in X time", they only have a "after X time" rather than "take X time" reading showing they are punctual.

(32) a. Carson arrived in two minutes/*for two minutes.

b. The bottle cracked in two minutes/*for two minutes.

Aspectual features of result verbs involving multiple-point scales are more complicated. On the one hand, as can be seen in (33)a when they are associated with the durative time adverbial "for X time", they are durative and atelic. On the other hand, when they are used with the frame time adverbial "in X time" in (33)b, they have a telic reading but with a "take X time" reading demonstrating durative aspectual feature typical of accomplishment verbs.

(33) a. The soup cooled for two minutes.

b. The soup cooled in two minutes. (i. e. reaching a desired temperature)

In summary, hallmarks of manner and result verbs are illustrated in the table below. In the following part, they will be used as criteria to judge the grammatical behaviors of the motion verbs in Mandarin so as to check the cross-linguistic validity of the MRC.

Table 2 Hallmarks of Manner and Result Verbs

Grammatical Behaviors	Type of Verbs	
	Manner verbs	Result verbs
Lexicalized component	Non-scalar change	Scalar change
Telicity	Atelic	Two-point scale: telic Multi-point scale: atelic/telic
Scale-denoting XP	Wide range	Very restricted
Object alternation	Allow unspecified/uncategorized	No unspecified/uncategorized

2.2.4 Disentangling Various Manners and Results

The notions of manner and result have been loosely described and used in research and different approaches use the notions in different ways. It is essential to make some clarification of them.

First, both manner and result meaning components are restricted only to lexical entailments which are constant in all uses of (a single sense of) a verb and which are distinct from contextual meaning inferred from specific uses of the verb with conventional implicature, from the selection of a particular noun phrase which fills in certain argument position or from the tense or aspectual feature that the verb associates with. For instance, as Rappaport Hovav and Levin (2010) argue the verbs wipe and scrub lexically specify actions with manners involving surface contact and motion, and in particular contexts these actions strongly implicate removing stuff from a surface, but as the implicated meaning can be explicitly cancelled, the removal meaning is not a lexical entailment of these verbs, as illustrated in (34).

(34) a. I scrubbed the tub for hours, but it didn't get any cleaner.

b. I just wiped the table, but none of the fingerprints came off.

(Rappaport Hovav, Levin, 2010)

Second, the semantic notion of manner as a non-scalar change should also be kept distinct from an adverbial manner which does not entail an independent change. For example, as argued by Rapapport Hovav (2008) though the word plunge has added conceptual components "quickly" and "abruptly", it is a directed motion verb, because the quick and abrupt manner entailed in the verb is only used in an adverbial sense to modify the directed motion and it does not encode an independent change itself. A similar example can also be found in Mandarin. The word 飞 fēi "fly" is said to entail the medium of traversal as air in its uses, and thus when used in the sense of "depart from a reference object" it is said to encode both the manner and direction of the motion. However, I argue that in this case the traversal medium of air is also used in an adverbial sense modifying the directed motion without encoding an independent change on its own and thus it encodes only one type of meaning component, the direction of motion.

Third, the manner is distinct from a notion of a relational manner. From a syntactic approach Mateu and Acedo-Matellan (2012) argue against the MRC suggest that even the most typical result verbs such as break can be used to specify the manner in some sentences such as "He broke into the room". According to them, the manner of break is read off from the syntactic configurat: an adjunct of the root to specifying the manner of getting into the room. However, Rapapport Hovav (2015) argues that "any root, whether result or manner, can in principle, be used as an event modifier", so in sentences like "He broke into the room" "The truth-conditional content or ontological type of break is still that of a result root, though in this case it specifies the manner of bringing about a different result". The misconception of the notion manner is one of the key reasons for different classifications of motion verbs in Mandarin. It will be further discussed in Chapter 3.

2.3 Arguments Against the MRC Hypothesis

Since the MRC hypothesis is claimed to be a general principal constraining the lexicalization patterns of the entire lexicon, it has generated much interest and controversy among researchers. In spite of much evidence for it, researchers have also put forward a variety of arguments against it. This section reviews arguments against the MRC hypothesis, re-examines the data these counterarguments are based on and reveals that these arguments do not pose real challenge for the MRC hypothesis. The counterarguments approach the issue from two different angles. Some researchers (Beavers, Koontz-Garboden, 2012; Goldberg, 2010) focusing on the lexical entailments of verbs propose some counterexample verbs which seem to encode both meaning components simultaneously in English. Other researchers (Mateu, Acedo-Matellán, 2012; Rapoport, 2012) reject a view of verb root of the MRC, i.e. whereas they admit there are linguistic phenomena corresponding to the MRC, they do not accept that it is held at the lexical level. Rather they either argue that it results from different syntactic configurations which verbs appear in or believe that it is reflected through the differences in aspectual focus. I will start with apparent counterexample verbs to the MRC and then move forward to arguments against the MRC as a lexical constraint.

2.3.1 Arguments Based on Counterexample Verbs in English

As noted by Husband (2011), the ultimate validity of the MRC rests on negative evidence. It is the lack of verbs which contain both meaning components that support the hypothesis. An obvious way to falsify the MRC is to name counterexamples. One group of alleged counterexample verbs to the MRC are so-called manner of killing verbs proposed by Beavers and Koontz-Garboden (2012) in (35).

(35) Manner of killing verbs:

   crucify, drown, electrocute, guillotine, hang

They develop a series of diagnostics for both a result and a manner component in a verb's meaning. Based on their tests, they claim these verbs to encode both meaning components violating the MRC. As to result components, using result denial tests "but nothing is different about X", object deletion tests and restricted resultative tests, they compare these verbs with canonical manner and result verbs and point out that these manner of killing verbs entail at least some result. For example, they illustrate with result denial tests and point out that these verb patterns with canonical result verbs such as break disallowing denial of result, are distinct from canonical manner verbs such as sweep without result entailments.

(36) a. Tracy swept the floor, but nothing is different about it.

   b. *Shane just broke the vase, but noting is about it.

   c. *Jane just drowned/hanged/crucified Joe, but nothing is different about him.

(Beavers, Koontz-Garboden, 2012)

Similarly, in object deletion tests, these verbs also show similar grammatical behaviors with result verbs such as shatter disallowing object deletion, different from manner verbs such as scrub, as illustrated in (37). These tests lead them to the conclusion that these verbs must entail result meaning components.

(37) a. All last night, Kim scrub.

　　b. *All last night Kim shattered.

　　c. *All last night Shane drowned/crucified/electrocuted.

(Beavers, Koontz-Garboden, 2012)

Likewise, using selectional restriction tests on subjects, denial of action and complexity of action tests, they conclude that the manner component in these verbs is also truth-conditionally entailed. For instance, these manner of killing verbs place selectional restriction on their subjects, patterning with other canonical manner verbs such as scrub and wipe in (38).

(38) a. The hammer broke/shattered the vase.

　　b. *The earthquake scrubbed/wiped the floor.

　　c. *The wind hang/crucify Jesus.

(Beavers, Koontz-Garboden, 2012)

In addition, based on denial of action tests these linguists also claim the manner component can be identified. Assuming causation is entailed in (39), they believe the ungrammatical status of the sentence is attributed to the contradiction between the entailed action in these verbs and the absence of action indicated in the context. Thus they summarize these verbs also lexicalize a manner component.

(39) * The governor crucified the prisoner, but didn't move a muscle—

　　rather, after taking office she failed to issue a pardon!

(Beavers, Koontz-Garboden, 2012)

In the following part, I will also have a close look at these verbs to check whether they lexicalize both meaning components simultaneously. A careful reanalysis of the actual uses of these verbs and the linguistic tests used by Beavers and Koontz-Garboden indicate that these verbs encode result but not manner and thus are merely result verbs.

Before the analysis of the actual uses of these verbs, it should be noted that not all manner of killing verbs proposed by Beavers and Koontz-Garboden are relevant to the MRC (Rappaport Hovav, 2015). While the MRC is considered in terms of its role in construction of verb meaning and verbs are often regarded as the default lexical unit the MRC applies to, it should be noted that the MRC is a lexical generalization about what is encoded in roots, which according to Rappaport Hovav and Levin (2010, 2015), are minimal meaningful elements of verbal meaning, but not verbs. Depending on what kind of lexical inventories and morphosyntactic structures available in a language, the grammatical unit of roots may or may not overlap with that of verbs. For example, in English many verbs such as run and wipe are mono-morpheme and thus the MRC applies to these monomorphemic verbs directly. However, as also noted by Rappaport Hovav and Levin (2010), in languages where verbs are productively formed by stems and affixes, the MRC only gets hold of the roots, the minimal meaningful lexical units rather than verbs. Therefore, one needs to be very cautious when judging whether a verb violates the MRC, since even in languages in which mono-morphemic verbs are the norm of the verbal construction, there may be verbs built on two or more morphemes or through morphological derivation. The apparent counterexamples electrocute and guillotine fall into this type. Obviously, electrocute is formed by combining the two morphemes, "electro-" and "execute". Guillotine is a denominal verb and the complexity of its meaning results from the complexity of the meaning related to the artifact noun it is derived from and from a rule of semantic interpretation accompanying morphological derivation (Kiparsky, 1997; Levin, Rappaport Hovav, 2015). Therefore, electrocute and guillotine do not strictly negate the MRC and the focus of the following discussion will be the three verbs crucify, drown and hang.

As to the meaning component of result of these verbs, Beavers and Koontz-Garboden state explicitly that they believe it to be "death", but they also argue that what result is encoded is not important, since their tests indicate these verbs at least entail some result. However, besides direct evidence for or against a lexical entailment of death in these verbs, it is also important to reveal the exact nature of result if they do entail this sense, because it will help to determine whether these verbs lexicalize an additional manner sense. First, contrary to Beavers and Koontz-Garboden's belief, it is shown that these verbs do not entail the meaning component of death. Researchers (Husband, 2011; Aldridge, 2012) notice that these verbs may be used in sentences where no death is entailed, as seen in (40). Though these verbs are conventionally associated with a result sense of death giving us a strong impression that these verbs always bring about death, conventional meaning is irrelevant to the present issue, and death is not their entailed meaning component.

(40) a. Ruben Enaje … is noted for being crucified 26 times … he has been crucified every year since 1985 on Good Friday.

b. A man hung himself by a belt in his closet … two days later he walked out of the hospital.

c. We did find some limited case studies of adults who drowned in cold water and who occasionally survived.

(Aldridge, 2012)

Then it leaves us to determine whether these verbs lexicalize other result components. Though death is not the entailed meaning component of these verbs, I agree with Beavers and Koontz-Garboden that these verbs do encode certain result. To be specific, I argue these verbs specify acquisition of a highly specific property denoted by the invariant component of meaning in the root. For example, the verb crucify must entail somebody's acquisition of a property "being hung up in a particular configuration". In fact, it is exactly the result the verb lexicalizes, namely, being nailed to a cross. Similarly, the verb drown entails an entity's acquisition of a property "being submerged in an ambient substance" (Rappaport Hovav, 2015). This is verified by the fact that though as discussed above the inferred death sense may be absent in some uses of these verbs, the meaning component concerning the acquisition of this highly specific property is constant across all uses of these verbs. As can be seen in (41), in the uses of these verbs, the acquisition of a kind of highly specific property by a theme denoted in the root cannot be cancelled.

(41) a. *The governor crucified the prisoner, but he was not nailed to
a cross.

b. *The governor hanged the prisoner, but he was not dropped
with a rope around his neck.

c. *The governor drowned the prisoner, but he was not submerged
in an ambient liquid substance.

As these verbs do encode the result component, it is no wonder that these
verbs pass the tests developed by Beavers and Koontz-Garboden aiming to identify
the result component of meaning. For example, the result denial test "nothing is
different from X" just indicates there is certain result, these verbs obviously will
be attested to pattern with canonical result verbs. The same is true for object
deletion tests. Since these verbs specify the acquisition of a new property by a
theme, as a structural argument of BECOME the theme must be syntactically
realized in line with the argument realization rule proposed by Rappaport Hovav
and Levin (1998).

Since these verbs do entail result, the remaining task is to show they do not
encode manner; otherwise they would be counterexamples to the MRC. In fact, if
the exact nature of result is clarified, it is not difficult to prove the manner is absent
in their lexical meaning. As discussed above, if the result meaning of these verbs is
acquisition of the highly specific property denoted by the root, then there is no
other meaning component encoded in these verbs. For example, as the verb hang
specifies the result as acquisition of a property of being dropped with a rope around
one's neck, then that is all about the lexical meaning and there is no additional
meaning component concerning manner.

However, Beavers and Koontz-Garboden claim these verbs must involve an
action by the agent, because using a negligence situation to deny an action (action
denial test) results in contradiction as illustrated in (39), repeated as (42) below.

(42) *The governor crucified the prisoner, but didn't move a muscle—

rather, after taking office she failed to issue a pardon!

(Beavers, Koontz-Garboden, 2012)

I argue that this test cannot be used to identify an action by the agent; rather it only proves that the external argument "the negligent governor" is not a proper causer for the result specified by these verbs. In other words, given the context of (42), a causative relation cannot be naturally constructed between the governor and the result that the prisoner was crucified. That's why (42) is contradictory. Note that Beavers and Koontz-Garboden assume with supporting context in (42) there is an entailed causation, but their assumption is not verified and even more seriously it is this assumption that makes them misidentify an action involved in these verbs. Neelman and Van de Koot (2010) argue that for an external argument to be a proper causer of an event, the external argument must be identified as the crucial contributing factor (CCF). They illustrate this notion as follows.

A speaker must decide which factor is essential in a causal relation (the CCF) and which factors fall in a ceteris paribus category. For example, suppose that several burglars use a hammer in an attempt to break a particularly strong window, and that only the most muscular of them—John—succeeds. This situation can be described by saying that John broke the window, where John is presented as the crucial contributory factor. It would be odd to say that the hammer broke the window. On the other hand, if John was alone and tried to break the window first by using a brick, then by using a piece of timber and finally by using a hammer, succeeding only in the last attempt, then the situation may be described quite naturally by saying that the hammer broke the window. In doing so, the choice of instrument is presented as the crucial contributory factor.

(Neelman, Van de Koot, 2010)

In addition, Neelman and Van de Koot also point out that for some causative verbs the intentionality of an external argument is critical for deciding whether the external argument can be regarded as the CCF, though the action by the external argument is irrelevant. For example, the verb murder, though as a result verb does not specify manner or means, it only selects an external argument with intentionality to be the CCF, as seen in (43).

(43) a. *The earthquake murdered the family.

b. *John murdered Mary by accident.

Verbs selecting an external argument with intentionality to be the CCF are incompatible with a causative relation resulting from negligence, since negligence is prototypically regarded as unintentional. However, as noted by Rappaport Hovav (2015), the transitive use of verbs electrocute and crucify in Beavers and Koontz-Garboden's example in particular predisposes the association of the verb with an external argument with intentionality. This is contradictory to the negligence situation. That's why (42) is unacceptable.

A more direct evidence for the absence of manner in these manner of killing verbs is that these verbs allow an inanimate subject, as seen in (44).

(44) a. Presumably one of [Basil] Clark's more imaginative underlings concocted the fiction that he had been buried up to his neck near the high tide point and left there for the rising sea to drown him ... **finally the waters drowned him**.

(Rappaport Hovav, 2015)

b. Without realizing that the cord had become wrapped around her neck, Mary jumped from the bridge, and **the cord snapped taut and hanged her**.

(Aldridge, 2012)

More significantly, the verbs drown and hang also participate in unaccusative-causative alternation, as in (45), though it is observed that verbs which impose restrictions on external arguments cannot be used in this way. This provides further evidence that these verbs do not specify any manner executed by an external argument.

> (45) a. The man drowned.
>
> b. At that time you could hang for stealing.

To summarize, Beavers and Koontz-Garboden's claim that some manner of killing verbs also lexicalize manner is merely an illusion. These verbs do not necessarily involve an action by the agent, and rather they only require external arguments with intentionality in their causative uses. Instead of posing selectional restrictions on subjects, with proper context these verbs allow inanimate subjects. Some of them also participate in causative-unaccusative alternation. Therefore, it is clear from the discussion above that these manner-of-killing verbs only encode result but not manner, and they are result verbs.

Focusing on purported counterexamples to the MRC proposed by Beavers and Koontz-Garboden, this section analyzes the actual uses of manner of killing words and argues that these verbs lexicalize only the result meaning component. Therefore, they do not pose real challenge for the MRC hypothesis.

2.3.2 Arguments Against the MRC as a Constraint Operating in the Lexicon

Other researchers admit that there are linguistic phenomena corresponding to the MRC, but they deny it as a principle operating in the lexicon. For example, Mateu and Acedo-Matellán (2012) argue the relevant linguistic phenomena corresponding to the MRC result from different syntactic configurations. Rapoport (2012) abandoning both the syntactic view of Mateu and Acedo-Matellán and a view of verb root of Rappaport Hovav and Levin argues that what the MRC reflects is just a switch in aspectual focus. Focusing on the counterarguments from the two approaches, this section re-examines the empirical evidence corresponding to the MRC and argues that semantic notions of manner and result based on the verb root are well motivated.

Mateu and Acedo-Matellán (2012) propose a syntactic approach to the MRC. According to these linguists, verb roots are not inherently typed as manner or result and the conceptual components encoded in verbs are not constrained in its complexity. Roots can integrate into syntactic structure in any way. The precise meaning of the verb in a sentence is determined by how and where the root is integrated into the syntactic structure. The MRC results from different configurations roots are associated with. A result sense is read off if a root appears as the predicate of a small clause through incorporation and a manner sense is interpreted if a root is an adjunct of verb. Since a root cannot possibly take two distinct positions in syntactic structure, the MRC follows.

Note that the lexicalist approach proposed by Rappaport Hovav and Levin (1995, 1998, 2010) and the syntactic approach adopted by Mateu and Acedo-Matellán (2012) are not completely incompatible. They share at least two points. First, the two approaches have a consensus on the bipartite nature of meaning, i.e. verb meaning components are made up of two parts: the structural meaning and idiosyncratic meaning. They all recognize that it is the structural meaning of a verb that affects a verb's argument realization patterns and other grammatical behaviors. Second, as to the MRC, they all adopt a verb root view that a root has only one position in certain structure ruling out the possibility that a verb root is associated with two positions simultaneously.

However, the two approaches also contrast with each other concerning the nature of the structural meaning. Rappaport Hovav and Levin consider the structural meaning to be represented as an event structure, which is determined by the semantics of the predicate, whereas Mateu and Acedo-Matellán argue the structural meaning is not determined by the lexical predicate but by syntactic constructions. In fact, it is just their different theoretical positions as to the nature of the structural meaning that make them to interpret the linguistic phenomena corresponding to the MRC differently. The evidence to support the syntactic approach is that the most prototypical result verb break can be interpreted as either a manner or result sense when it takes different positions in the syntactic structure, as in (46).

(46) a. He broke into the room. [$_{VP}$ [$_v$ √BREAK v] [$_{SC}$ [$_{DP}$ he] [into the room]]]

  b. The glass broke. [$_{VP}$ v [$_{SC}$ [$_{DP}$ the glass] [√BREAK]]]

(Mateu, Acedo-Matellan, 2012)

Nonetheless, Rappaport Hovav (2015) argues that the meaning component of manner should be differentiated from the relational notion of manner, as in principle both manner and result roots may be used as event modifiers representing the relational manner as in (46)a. In this case, though the root is used to modify the whole event, its truth conditional content/ontological type is still that of the result. She further explains that a verb root sometimes can be used to modify an event type which it is not prototypically associated with. An example Rappaport Hovav provides is the way construction which describes moving along a path in a particular manner. It has been observed by linguists (e.g. Goldberg, 1995; Jakendoff, 1997) that verbs in this construction in their unmarked uses do not normally select the way complement and they are often manner verbs, but sometimes result verbs can also be used, as in (47).

(47) The woman's 13-year-old, who broke his way out to safety, says he woke up to find his whole house on fire.

(Rappaport Hovav, 2015)

As to this case, though the result verb break is used to modify a transitional motion which is different from the change encoded in its lexical meaning, the truth conditional content or the ontological type remains unchanged, namely, a result one.

In addition, concerning the problems that the syntactic approaches to argument realization face in general, Kiparsky (1997) points out that even a pure syntactic structure has to make crucial reference to conceptual knowledge and thus requires a semantic representation of the predicate. For instance, in Mateu and Acedo-Matellán's analysis of the manner-of-killing verb guillotine, they argue the syntactic argument structure of the verb in (48)a corresponds to its use as a causative predicate of change-of-state as in (48)b. In this case the root is the complement of an abstract P element that expresses "Terminal Coincidence Relation"①. However, they also explain that structurally nothing prevents (48)a from being interpreted as involving a structure like (48)c; rather it is just pragmatically ill-formed. In a sense, by saying this they admit that the semantics of the predicate is important to constrain which syntactic structure it may be associated with.

(48) a. They guillotined Mary.

b. [$_{VP}$ [$_{DP}$ They] [$_{v'}$ √ GUILLOTINE [$_{PP=SC}$ [$_{DP}$ Mary] [$_{P'}$ P$_{TCR}$ √ GUILLOTINE]]]]

c. # [$_{VP}$ [$_{DP}$ They] $_{[v'}$ [$_{v}$ √GUILLOTINE v] $_{[DP}$ Mary]]]

(# on the reading: "They created Mary guillotining/with a guillotine.")

In fact, the semantics of the predicate guillotine provides essential reference for proper syntactic structures to be built. As Kiparsky (1997) notes denomial causative verbs refer to generically intentional activities and if an action is named after a thing, it involves a canonical use of the thing. Thus the verb guillotine derives its prototypical meaning from the canonical use of the thing that it is named after, i.e. a piece of machine used to cut off people's head. Only based on this conceptual component of the predicate, may the selection of relevant syntactic structures be possible. Similarly, Rappaport Hovav also observes that even the syntactic approach makes implicit distinction between conceptual and relational notion of manner representing the former as (49)a and the latter as (49)b. More essentially, as proposed by Rappaport Hovav and Levin (2010), the semantics of manner and result verbs can be well delineated as scalar and non-scalar changes independently, so it is possible to tease the lexicalized meaning components of verb roots out from those contributed by particular contexts.

---

① In Hale and Kayser's 2002 sense: A TCR involves a coincidence between one edge or terminus of the theme's path and the place, while a central coincidence relation (CCR) involves a coincidence between the center of the theme and the center of the place.

(49) a. [$_{v'}$ [$_v$ √SMILE] [√SMILE]]]

    b. [$_{v'}$ [$_v$ √SMILE v] [$_{DP}$ their thanks]]]

Therefore, it can be seen that conceptual knowledge is indispensable in explaining the notions of manner and result, and they cannot be reduced to merely different syntactic configurations.

Rapoport (2012) proposes the MRC derives from differences in aspectual focus rejecting a root view of the MRC proposed by both Rappaport Hovav and Levin as well as by Mateu and Acedo-Matellán. According to her, the minimal semantic unit which determines the syntactic structure that a verb may appear in is not the root; rather a verb may be composed of two different types of atomic meaning components, manner atoms (manners, instruments, means) and result atoms (states, locations), which freely and independently merge syntactic structures with different argument realization patterns and aspectual properties. Variable grammatical behaviors of a verb are all derived from a single lexical entry. A manner or a result atom projecting distinct aspectual features each is associated with only one part of a syntactic structure. When we interpret a structure, only one part of the structure can be foregrounded with the other being backgrounded. The impossibility of foregrounding the two parts of a structure simultaneously results in the MRC.

In Rapoport's approach, verbs with variable grammatical behaviors can be explained directly by the free projection of different atomic meaning components into syntactic structures, so it does not have the problem of the proliferation of lexical entries on the one hand, and on the other hand, it also saves the trouble of formulating interfaces or mapping rules such as template augmentation based on event structures. In a sense, it is theoretically economical and effective in tackling the lexicon and syntax interface. However, there is also an obvious problem with it: free projection of meaning atoms and proposed aspectual focus lead to undergeneralization of verbs which otherwise fall into natural classes based on their ontological type, manner or result. According to Rapoport (2012), based on how verbs are composed of different types of atomic meaning components, they can be divided into three types: verbs with a manner atom, verbs with a result atom and verbs with both manner and result atoms, as in (50).

> (50) a. Verbs with a manner atom: run, jump, laugh
>
>   b. Verbs with a result atom: arrive, enter, advance, cool, melt
>
>   c. Verbs with both manner and result atoms: cut, melt, break, hit

As to verbs with only one type of atomic meaning components either manner (50)a or result (50)b, there is no disagreement upon the interpretation of grammatical behaviors of these verbs between Rappaport Hovav and Levin's lexicalist approach and Rapoport's atom theory, since no matter how the meaning unit is named, manner/result atoms or manner/result verb roots, their different grammatical behaviors are basically determined by the meaning components encoded in the lexical entries. The two approaches do show contrast in interpreting grammatical behaviors of verbs which are claimed to have both types of meaning atoms in Rapoport's approach in (50)c. It can be seen that these verbs crosscut the ontological types of manner and result verbs in lexicalist approach. Rapoport mainly bases her argument on verbs which show the grammatical behaviors of both manner and result verbs. Generally, she considers the properties of verbs that can appear with constructions or time adverbials which show the durative aspectual feature as hallmarks to indicate they contain manner atoms. According to her, for example, concerning the meaning atoms that the verb cut contains, whereas generally its result atom is focused to indicate a result state of a clear separation in its prototypical uses as in (51)a, it is also possible to focus its manner atom when it is used in a progressive aspect, with durative time adverbial, or in conative construction in (51)b-(51)d. Rapoport explains that in either case both meaning atoms are present, but only one can be focused at a time.

> (51) a. Jane cut the ropes in ten minutes.
>
>   b. Jane was cutting the bread for an hour.
>
>   c. Jane cut the ropes for ten minutes.

d. Jane cut at the ropes for an hour.

(Rapoport, 2012)

Rappaport Hovav and Levin (2014) also address the variable behaviors of the verb cut proposing it lexicalize only one meaning component manner or result in each use with the other one dropping out. Probably, at this stage it is difficult to tell which approach is more tenable.

However, some other verbs which are also claimed to contain both manner and result atoms, such as hit and break, pose a challenge for Rapoport's atom theory, because these verbs never defocus the meaning atom that is assumed to be the lexicalized meaning component in the roots in Rappaport Hovav and Levin's (1998, 2010) approach and alternatively focus the other meaning atom. For instance, Rapoport claims that break contains both a result atom "being dysfunctional" and a manner atom "using forceful means" (Rapoport, 2012), but in its various uses, the manner atom cannot be focused. Using Rapoport's tests to detect the aspectual focus associated with the manner atom, break cannot be used in conative construction as in (52)a and it is incompatible with durative time adverbials as in (52)b. Similarly, the verb hit is also assumed to have both a manner atom "using forceful manner" and a result atom "being at the point of contacting" (Rapoport, 2012), but it does not exhibit the aspectual focus of the result atom, as it is not compatible with framed time adverbial "in X time" as in (52)c. Then if these verbs contain a type of meaning atoms which cannot be aspectually focused, how could one possibly know there is indeed such a meaning atom in the semantics of the lexical entries? Rapoport proposes that only the manner atom associated with "wielding of a particular instrument" can be focused (Rapoport, 2012), and there is no focusable action associated with "implementing forceful means", but the fact is that though both the verb break and the verb hit are associated with a manner atom "forceful means/manner", the action expressed by hit in (52)d but not by break in (52)a can be focused. Therefore Rapoport's argument that verbs such as break and hit contain two types of meaning atoms are not convincing; rather these facts are better to be understood as these verbs contain only one meaning component result or manner, thus conforming to their ontological categorization suggested by Rappaport Hovav and Levin (1998, 2010). Correspondingly, it is also better to treat verbs like cut as polysemous verbs with different meaning components lexicalized in each use. It is more tenable to regard the MRC as a constraint operating in the lexicon rather than differences in aspectual focus projected from different meaning atoms.

(52) a. *Jane broke at the vase.

b. *Jane broke the vase for two minutes

c. * Jane hit the door in a minute.

d. Jane hit at the door.

This section has examined arguments which question the validity of the MRC as a lexical constraint. It reveals that manner and result cannot be reduced to either different syntactic configurations or differences in aspectual focus. A root view of the MRC that manner and result are conceptual notions constrained by verbs' ontological type is supported.

2.4 Summary

This chapter has reviewed the lexicalist approach to the lexicon and syntax interface and the theoretical framework related to the MRC which has been explicated by introducing the theoretical motivation for the MRC hypothesis, semantic notions of the manner and result verbs and hallmarks of the two types of verbs. Manner of killing verbs in English, which are proposed to constitute counterexample verbs to the MRC, are discussed and demonstrate that they actually lexicalize only the meaning component of result but not manner and thus do not undermine the validity of the MRC. Two approaches that observe the linguistic phenomena corresponding to the MRC but deny its status as a lexical constraint are also reviewed and show that the MRC cannot be understood as only deriving from different syntactic configurations or merely differences in aspectual focus. Rather it is a viable principle operating in the lexicon.

Chapter ③

The Manner/Result
Complementarity
in Modern Chinese

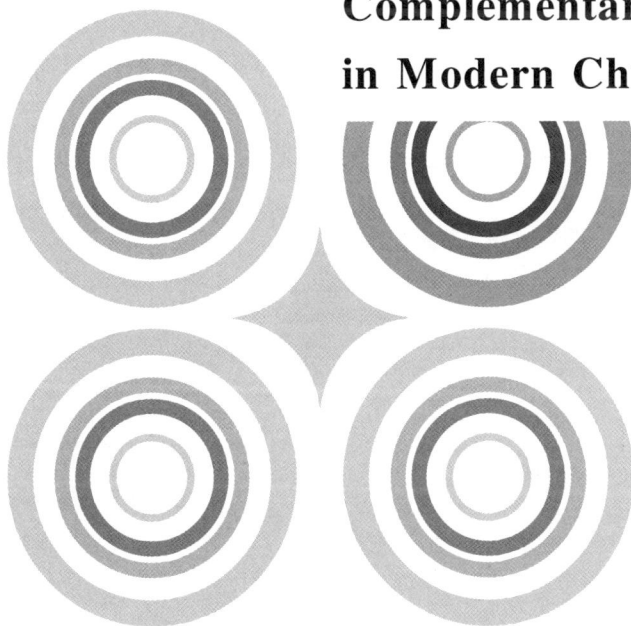

This chapter investigates the cross-linguistic validity of the MRC hypothesis by looking at the motion verbs in Modern Chinese. Firstly, previous studies of classification of Chinese motion verbs will be reviewed. In addition, based on an analysis of motion verbs collected by Chen and Guo (2009), general lexicalization patterns of Chinese motion verbs will be looked at with a focus on controversies over the classification of motion verbs and potential counterexamples to the MRC. I will also have a close look at three motion verbs 走 zǒu "walk", 跑 pǎo "run" and 飞 fēi "fly", which are all classified as manner verbs by scholars, but seem to be counterexamples to the MRC as they can also encode result meaning components when used in some constructions. I suggest that though these verbs can lexicalize both the manner and result meaning component, they never lexicalize both meaning components simultaneously in actual uses and thus conform to the MRC. On the contrary, they further support the cross-linguistic validity of the MRC.

3.1 Previous Studies of Classification of Modern Chinese Motion Verbs

As discussed in Chapter 1, concerning a motion event encoding the typological status of Chinese is controversial. Though Talmy (1985, 2000, 2009) classifies Chinese as a satellite-framed language, there are different voices which tend to group Chinese as a verb-framed language (Tai, 2003) or an equipollently-framed language (Slobin, 2004, 2006). One of the reasons for this controversy is that researchers hold different views on the lexicalized meaning components in Chinese motion verbs and their corresponding grammatical status. There is a consensus that there are both manner-of-motion verbs and directed motion verbs in Modern Chinese, but as to the classification of specific verbs, scholars provide different solutions.

In traditional studies of Chinese motion constructions (e.g. Chao, 1968; Jiang, Wu, 1997; Liu, 1998), verbs which can be used as the second and the third verb in directional verbal constructions have been the focus of the research. As all these verbs can follow another motion verb to specify the direction of motion, they have been dubbed as directional complements (DC) by scholars. For example, in (53)a the verb 上 shàng "ascend" is regarded as a directional complement specifying the direction of motion, as along with the action of walking, the theme ends up at the specific location "up to the second floor". Besides being used as directional complements, most verbs of this type can also be used alone as the main verb of a sentence to indicate the direction of motion, as in (53)b.

(53) a. 他　走　　上　　　了　　二　楼。

　　　　 tā　zǒu　shàng　le　èr　lóu

　　　　 he　**walk**　**ascend**　ASP　two　building

　　　　 "He walked up to the second floor."

　　　 b. 他　上　　　了　　二　楼。

　　　　 tā　shàng　le　èr　lóu

　　　　 he　**ascend**　ASP　two　building

　　　　 "He ascended to the second floor."

There are some differences that distinguish their uses as directional complements like (53)a from their other uses as main path verbs like (53)b. For example, in the cases where they are used as directional complements, they are read in neutral tone and have reduced arguments. However, since they express similar conceptual meaning, they are generally considered to share the same verbal root in both cases. For instance, no matter whether it is used as a directional complement or as a main verb, the verb 来 lái "come" expresses the same meaning, i.e. a motion event towards a deictic center typically anchored at the location of the speaker. In the former case like (53)a, the directional complements usually appear alongside with two types of verbs in Chinese, verbs that describe the manner of motion (e.g. 跳 tiào "jump", 滚 gǔn "roll" and 流 liú "flow") and verbs that describe physical action which results in a caused motion in the patient (e.g. 抬 tái "lift", 搬 bān "move", 扔 rēng "throw"). However, these verbs only describe the cause or manner of the motion and neither of them specifies the direction of motion.

Motion verbs which can be used as directional complements are listed in (54). These verbs can be further divided into two subtypes based on whether they indicate a direction with reference to the speaker or a deictic center based on a landmark in the discourse. There are only two members of the former type: 来 lái "come" and 去 qù "go" and all the others belong to the latter type.

(54) Deictic DCs:

		Non-deictic DCs:			
来,	去	上,	下,	进,	出
lái	qù	shàng	xià	jìn	chū
"come"	"go"	"ascend"	"descend"	"enter"	"exit"
		起,	回,	过,	开
		qǐ	huí	guò	kāi
		"rise up"	"return"	"pass"	"away"

Thus in traditional studies of Chinese motion constructions, as a rule of thumb, verbs that can be used as directional complements are considered as directed motion verbs to encode the direction of motion, and the verbs that the directional complements follow are just regarded as manner verbs in general to indicate the cause or manner of the motion.

However, there are problems with this traditional classification. Though in Modern Chinese, to express self-agentive motion events, the direction of motion is often indicated by these verbs as directional complements like (53)a or as main verbs like (53)b, in caused-motion constructions, following transitive action verbs, some other verbs also seem to encode the direction of motion. For example, in (55)a and (55)c the verbs 落 luò "fall" and 退 tuì "recede", following transitive action verbs 吹 chuī "blow" and 打 dǎ "beat" respectively, also seem to indicate the direction of motion. Moreover, as illustrated in (55)b and (55)d, in other cases these verbs can also be followed by the prototypical directional complements mentioned above. In other words, the positions of these verbs are quite flexible: they may follow other action verbs on the one hand, and on the other hand they may be followed by other directional complements.

(55) a. 秋风　　　　　**吹**　**落**　了　　树叶。
　　　qiūfēng　　　**chuī**　**luò**　le　　shùyè
　　　autumn wind　**blow**　**fall**　ASP　tree leaf
　　　"The autumn wind blew the leaves off."

　　b. 苹果　　从　树　上　**落**　下　　来。
　　　píngguǒ　cóng　shù　shang　**luò**　xià　　lai
　　　apple　　from　tree　LOC　**fall**　descend　come
　　　"The apple fell off from the tree."

　　c. 项羽　　**打**　**退**　了　　秦军。
　　　Xiàng Yǔ　**dǎ**　**tuì**　le　　Qín jūn
　　　Xiang Yu　**beat**　**retreat**　ASP　Qin army
　　　"Xiang Yu beat the army of Qin back."

　　d. 敌人　**退**　**回**　去　了。
　　　dírén　**tuì**　**huí**　qù　le
　　　enemy　**recede**　**return**　go　ASP
　　　"The enemy receded."

As to their flexible positions in directional constructions some questions naturally arise—What meaning components do these verbs encode? Do they encode two types of meaning components together or do they have different lexicalized meanings corresponding to their different positions in the directional constructions?

The traditional classification of motion verbs does not seem to provide satisfactory answers to these questions.

Influenced by Talmy's well-known classification of motion verbs based on what semantic component—path vs. manner—is conflated into the verb, another approach to the lexicalization patterns of Chinese motion verbs has been based on Talmy's framework. Lamarre (2008) points out that the group of verbs called directional complements are only a small part of path verbs in Chinese. Whether a verb can be used as the directional complement is also determined by the degree of grammaticalization a verb has undergone. Only those verbs that have been grammaticalized as satellites may follow verbs expressing the manner or cause of motion to be used as directional complements. She also names some verbs which she believes to encode path but cannot be used as path satellites such as 升 shēng "rise", 沉 chén "sink", 钻 zuān "make one's way into", 退 tuì "retreat" and 穿 chuān "pass through". Chen and Guo (2009) also study the lexicalization patterns of Chinese motion events under Talmy's framework. Though they overtly express that "manner verbs refer to the way in which a figure carries out a motion" and "path verbs refer to trajectory over which a figure moves, typically with respect to another reference object" (Chen, Guo, 2009), they seem to adopt the traditional way of classification of motion verbs in their actual studies. The verbs categorized as path ones are practically restricted to those which are prototypical directional complements. Contrastively, those verbs which can be followed by directional complements, i.e. those pose problematic verbs for traditional studies such as 落 luò "fall", 掉 diào "fall", etc., are all classified as manner verbs, opposite to Lamarre's (2008) view. Different from both Lamarre (2008) and Guo and Chen (2009), Hsiao (2009) regards the same group of verbs as verbs encoding both manner and path information. Based on detailed studies of the conceptual components lexicalized in manner-of-motion verbs, she explains that verbs such as 掉 diào "fall" and 沉 chén "sink" encode both manner and path meaning components, since they all lexicalize a direction with reference to the gravity and some conceptual property characterized as a manner, for example, force or medium of motion. Though these studies are all under Talmy's framework, there are still controversies over the classification of some motion verbs.

Lin (2011) points out that these controversies result from the lack of consistent criteria to determine the ontological categorization of verbs, since in these studies motion verbs are classified primarily via an intuition-based semantic grouping. That's why in Guo and Chen's (2009) study, 钻 zuān "squeeze" and 掉 diào "fall" are classified as manner-of-motion verbs but as directed motion verbs in Lamarre (2008). Still, Hsiao (2009) regards verbs such as 掉 diào "fall" and 沉 chén "sink" encoding both manner and path. Ma (2008) and Shi and Wu (2014) also name 登 dēng "mount" as lexicalizing both manner and path. It is necessary to reexamine the classification of Chinese motion verbs based on systematic and consistent criteria.

Based on the lexical property of manner and result verbs suggested by Rappaport Hovav and Levin (2010), Lin (2011) introduces a series of tests to identify manner or direction of motion verbs via their syntactic distribution. For example, according to Lin (2011), manner and direction of motion verbs exhibit different compatibility with other elements expressing manner or result: only manner-of-motion verbs are compatible with a variety of result and path phrases and only directed motion verbs can be modified by various manner adverbials or manner verbs. As illustrated in (56), 跳 tiào "jump" as a manner verb is compatible with a variety of path and result phrases such as 断腿 duàn tuǐ "break legs". Nevertheless, it cannot be modified by adverbials or verbs expressing other manners such as 滚 gǔn "roll" or 爬 pá "crawl".

(56) a. 他　跳　　出　了　　水坑。

　　　tā　tiào　chū　le　　shuǐkēng

　　　he　**jump　exit**　ASP　puddle

　　　"He jumped out of the puddle."

(Cited in Peck et al. (2013))

　　b. 他　跳　　断　　了　　腿。

　　　tā　tiào　duàn　le　　tuǐ

he **jump break** ASP leg

"His leg was broken as a result of his jumping."

c. *他　滚/爬　　　跳。

　　tā　gǔn/pá　tiào

　　he　roll/crawl　jump

　　"He jumped by rolling/crawling." (Intended meaning)

However, directed motion verbs show contrastive grammatical behaviors. For example, directed motion verb 回 huí "return", as illustrated by Lin (2011) in (57), can be modified by a variety of manner verbs such as 滚 gǔn "roll" and 跳 tiào "jump", but it is incompatible with path or result phrases which are not related to the path lexicalized in the verb itself.

(57) a. 敌人　跳/滚　　着　回　　关外。

　　dírén　tiào/gǔn　zhe　huí　guānwài

　　enemy **jump/roll DUR return** pass.outside

　　"The enemy returned to the outside of the pass jumping/rolling."

(Cited in Lin (2011))

b. *敌人　回　累　　了。

　　dírén　huí　léi　le

　　enemy **return be.tired** ASP

　　"The enemy became tired as a result of returning." (Intended meaning)

As can be seen in the above examples, linguistic tests introduced by Lin (2011) can distinguish manner-of-motion verbs and directed motion verbs in Chinese in a consistent manner so far. However, there are also problems with Lin's tests. First, though the manner and result meaning components can be tested through compatibility tests, she does not clarify the exact nature of manner or result encoded in Chinese motion verbs, so the notions of manner and result need more elaboration. Second, in her tests, the aspectual features of two different types of verbs are not taken into consideration. This makes the test incomplete and may leave the ontological categorization of some verbs inaccurate. Third, some motion verbs with inconsistent grammatical behaviors are neglected. For example, the verbs 走 zǒu "walk", 跑 pǎo "run" and 飞 fēi "fly" are all classified as manner-of-motion verbs, but they also seem to encode a directed motion sense when used in some constructions. The lexicalized meaning components and grammatical behaviors of these verbs need further examination. In the following part, I will further clarify the notions of manner and result in Chinese motion events and reexamine the lexicalization patterns of Chinese motion verbs based on sample verbs collected by Chen and Guo (2009) so as to give a more comprehensive analysis of Chinese motion verbs.

3.2 Notions of Manner and Result in Chinese Motion Events

Both the notions of manner and result in Chinese motion events can be further elaborated with subcomponents which make up these two relatively abstract and general terms, but as far as a motion verb's grammatical behavior is concerned, some subcomponents (e. g. medium of motion) cannot be used as criteria to determine a verb's ontological type as manner or result. Assuming verbs in motion domain parallel to those in the change-of-state domain, verbs indicating concepts of manner and path of motion are subtypes of manner and result verbs in general respectively. However, the notions of manner and path in motion events are not clearly delineated. Talmy (1985, 2000) considers manner as an additional but conceptually abstract activity that the figure of the motion event exhibits. He states that "manner refers to a subsidiary action or state that a patient manifests concurrently with its main action or state" (Talmy, 2000). He explains the manner encoded in the English verb float as an example. In the sentence "The balloon floated into the church.", besides the main action "move", a subsidiary action "floating in the process" is indicated as a manner by the verb. However, other researchers (Narasimhan, 1998; Pourcel, 2006; Hsiao, 2009) argue that the notion of manner contains a range of subcomponents which needs finer elaboration. Slobin (2004) proposes that manner covers "an ill-defined set of dimensions that modulate motion, including motor pattern, rate, rhythm, posture, affect, and evaluative factors". Some semantic categories decomposed by Slobin (2006) are provided in (58).

> (58) a. Motor pattern: hop, jump, skip
>
> b. Rate of motion: walk, run, sprint
>
> c. Force dynamics: step, tread, tramp
>
> d. Attitude: amble, saunter, stroll

Slobin's decomposition of the conceptual properties related to manner certainly provides us with a better understanding of the dimensions that manner is constructed on. The conceptualization of each manner verb is better characterized. For example, as run and walk demonstrate differences in the rate of motion, in prototypical cases the rate of run is conceived to be higher than that of walk. However, the specific manner related to a verb may reflect a collective property represented by several subcomponents, and each single property itself may not be grammatical relevant. For example, besides the rate differences between run and walk, their gait patterns are also distinct from each other, but in spite of their differences in the nuanced conceptual properties of manner, run and walk show similar grammatical behaviors. Jackendoff (2002) also makes similar observation and argues that the semantic nuances that distinguish verbs like walk, jog, limp, strut, and shuffle are best left to the modality-specific sensorimotor system.

The difference between varied ways of conceptualization of the notion is a result of different theoretical orientations. Talmy is not concerned with the specific conceptual components of manner; rather he abstracts them as a cover term in contrast with the notion of path in motion events. Researchers such as Slobin (2004) and Hsiao (2009) try to describe the range of conceptual components that make up Talmy's cover term. Rappaport Hovav and Levin (1998, 2010) are not interested in specific concepts related to manner either; they pay particular attention to those

汉语位移动词中的方式结果互补性研究——共时与历时视角

| | | | | | | | | | | | | The Manner/Result Complementarity in Chinese Motion Verbs: Synchronic and Diachronic Perspectives

meaning components which affect the grammatical behaviors, especially the argument realization of verbs. The notion of manner only reflects the ontological type of a verb and determines the way the verb associates with event templates. The details of conceptual components such as "contact" "medium" and "force" are merely idiosyncratic meaning components which distinguish verbs within an ontological type. Because in many cases they are not grammatically relevant, the specific natures of them are not of primary concern.

Path in Talmy's term is also an abstract semantic-conceptual notion: the trajectory over which an entity moves typically with respect to a reference object. According to Talmy (2000), path has three main components: the vector, the conformation and the deictic component. The vector expresses the sense in which the relation between Figure and Ground is established. There are mainly three types of path indicated by the vector: departure, arrival and traversal. The conformation creates a geometrical shaping of the ground. The deictic component conveys whether the sense of the path is towards the speaker or away from the speaker. The notion of result in the motion domain proposed by Rappaport Hovav and Levin (2010) is consistent with Talmy's notion of path. The path information indicated by the vector and the conformation corresponds to the direction of motion with respect to certain reference object. Similarly the path information expressed by the vector and the deictic element corresponds to the context-determined direction of motion. Rappaport Hovav and Levin also consider path involving a scale, which is made up of three components: dimension, values and ordering relation (Fleischhauer, Gamerschlag, 2014). The components can also be delineated by Talmy's three components of path.

Manner and result in Chinese motion events can also be characterized by conceptual components that make up these notions. For example, with reference to the conceptual components associated English manner verbs, Hsiao (2009) explores the range of conceptual components that make up the notion of manner in Chinese manner verbs. Based on her analysis, English and Chinese lexicalize similar conceptual components in manner verbs (e.g. medium, contact, force and rate). However, it needs to be noted that in terms of ontological type of a motion verb as a manner or path, some conceptual components may not be attributed to a conceptual property to differentiate the two notions. For example, the English verbs fall and drop are claimed to encode the force of gravity as a conceptual property of manner. Likewise, in the verb sink, a conceptual property associated with medium of motion is argued to be lexically specified. Because the force of gravity is practically involved and omnipresent in all motions and it is often used as reference or ground information of the motion, though it is more salient in some verbs than others, the force of gravity alone may not be regarded as a contrastive conceptual property determining whether the verb involves manner or not. The same is true for the conceptual property of medium of motion. In fact, this observation is supported by the grammatical behaviors of these verbs, since they completely conform to the hallmarks of result verbs. Therefore, verbs only encode the gravity force or medium of motion are not regarded as a specified manner in the lexical meaning. It also applies to Chinese motion verbs such as 掉 diào "fall", 沉 chén "sink", 落 luò "fall", and their ontological categorization and grammatical behaviors will also be analyzed in the following part.

3.3 Re-examination of the Lexcialization Patterns of Chinese Motion Verbs

3.3.1 A Preliminary Distinction

Though languages vary in the tendency to encode path or manner into the verb, both manner-of-motion and directed motion verbs exist in almost every language. It's a good way to reexamine the grammatical behaviors of the manner-of-motion and directed motion verbs collected and analyzed by scholars in previous studies so as to check whether these verbs show hallmarks of manner or result verbs and testify the validity of the MRC hypothesis. Among the studies, Chen and Guo (2009) provide an extensive and representative sample of motion verbs collected from nine novels. In this section, I will use Chen and Guo's sample verbs as a basis to reexamine the grammatical behaviors of Chinese motion verbs, to look at the controversies over the classification of some verbs and some potential counterexamples to the MRC.

My tests for manner and path components lexicalized in motion verbs are partly based on Lin's tests. However, I will also take the aspectual property of the manner and direction of motion verbs into account, as different aspectual features of manner and result verbs are also crucial to their syntactic distributions. As discussed in Chapter 2, Rapapport Hovav and Levin (2010) suggest distinct scalar notions underlying manner and result verbs. In the case of motion verbs, manner-of-motion verbs encode non-scalar changes, so they are atelic. Directed motion verbs can be further divided into two subtypes depending on whether they entail two-point or multi-point scalar changes: verbs lexicalizing two-point scalar changes are necessarily telic and punctual, and verbs lexicalizing multi-point scales have either telic or atelic readings depending on the contexts.

Chen and Guo (2009) collect 59 motion verbs altogether: 41 manner verbs, 6 neutral verbs and 12 path verbs. Since neutral verbs such as 站 zhàn "stand" do not encode the motion meaning on their own and only acquire the notion of motion when combined with other path verbs, they are not regarded as inherent motion verbs and thus are excluded from the present study.

Among all the other verbs, there is no controversy over the status of the 12 path verbs, which are listed in (59), as their grammatical behaviors clearly conform to the hallmarks of result verbs. For example, the sentence in (60) shows that the verb 到 dào "arrive" lexicalizes the direction of motion as arriving a goal of motion, so it requires the reference object serving as the goal of the motion to be explicitly expressed, but it is incompatible with the source reference 从北京 cóng Běijīng "from Beijing".

(59) Path/Directed motion verbs:

来 lái "come"	去 qù "go"
到 dào "arrive"	回 huí "return"
进 jìn "enter"	出 chū "exit"
过 guò "cross"	下 xià "descend"
上 shàng "ascend"	开 kāi "part"
离 lí "leave/part"	入 rù "enter"

倒 dǎo "fall down"

(Chen, Guo, 2009)

(60) *他 从　　北京　　 到　　了。

　　　tā cóng Běijīng dào le

　　　he from Beijing go ASP

　　　"#He arrived from Beijing."

The incompatibility between the verb 到 dào "arrive" and the prepositional phrase 从北京 cóng Běijīng "from Beijing" indicates that the goal path is the lexicalized meaning component in the verb, which cannot be violated.

Moreover, these directed motion verbs cannot take either other scale-denoting phrases or unsubcategorized objects as their complements. As illustrated by examples in (61)a and (61)b, the verb 进 jìn "enter" cannot take either 累 lèi "tired" or 一身灰 yì shēn huī "his whole body covered with dust" as its complements or objects. In contrast, since directed motion verbs do not specify the manner in which the motion is carried out, they are compatible with verbs which describe varied manner information. The example in (61)c shows that verb 进 jìn "enter" is compatible with various manners, as it only lexicalizes a path which ends inside of some space but not how the motion is carried out.

(61) a. *他 进　　门　　 进　　累　　 了。

　　　　tā jìn mén jìn lèi le

　　　　he enter door enter tired ASP

　　　　"He became tired as a result of entering the door." (Intended meaning)

　　b. *他 进　　门　　 进　　了　　 一　　身　　 灰。

　　　　tā jìn mén jìn le yī shēn huī

　　　　he enter door enter ASP one body dust

　　　　"He entered the door making his whole body covered with

dust." (Intended meaning)

c. 他 跳/走/跑 进 房间。

Tā tiào/zǒu/pǎo jìn fángjiān

He jump/walk/run enter room

"He jumped/walked/ran into the room."

In addition, based on what kind of scale these directed motion verbs involve, two-point or multi-point scale, they also conform to the aspectual features of result verbs. For example, involving two-point scale, 到 dào "arrive", 出 chū "exit", and 进 jìn "enter" are punctual and telic, and thus they are not compatible with durative time adverbial as the sentence in (62)a shows. However, involving multi-point scale, 来 lái "come", 去 qù "go", 回 huí "return", 上 shàng "ascend" and 下 xià "descend" can be either telic or atelic. The example in (62)b shows that 上 shàng "ascend" has an atelic reading when it appears with durative time adverbial 一个小时 yìgè xiǎoshí "for an hour", but in (62)c it has a telic reading when used with a frame time adverbial 一分钟内 yì fēnzhōng nèi "in a minute".

(62) a. *他 到 家 到 了 一 个 小时。

tā dào jiā dào le yī gè xiǎoshí

he arrive home arrive ASP one CL hour

\# "He arrived home for an hour."

b. 他 上 山 上 了 一 个 小时。

tā shàng shān shàng le yī gè xiǎoshí

he ascend hill ascend ASP one CL hour

"He climbed the hill for an hour."

c. 他 一 分钟 内 就 上 了 五 楼。

tā yī fēnzhōng nèi jiù shàng le wǔ lóu

he one minute within already ascend ASP five floor

"He ascended to the fifth floor in a minute."

Thus it can be seen that directed motion verbs also show distinct aspectual features of manner verbs. Whereas manner verbs always show atelic aspectual features, directed motions verbs can gain telic readings even without supporting contexts.

Though the lexicalized meaning and grammatical behaviors of directed motion verbs are quite homogeneous and straightforward, verbs which are classified as manner-of-motion verbs by Chen and Guo (2009) seem to be more complicated, as their categorizations are controversial and it is not so easy to determine their ontological type. In comparison with other related studies. I divide them into four groups which are listed in (63), namely, (63)a uncontroversial manner-of-motion verbs, (63)b verbs which are categorized as manner verbs by Chen and Guo, but as directed motion verbs by other scholars, (63)c verbs which are claimed to encode both manner and result meaning components by some scholars and (63)d verbs which are all categorized as manner-of-motion verbs in previous studies but I observe that they lexicalize directed motion when used in some constructions. In the remainder of this section, I will look at these four types of verbs to examine the grammatical behaviors of uncontroversial verbs in group (63)a, to clarify the ontological status of verbs in group (63)b seeking possible reasons for the controversy over their classification, and to check whether verbs in group (63)c indeed encode both manner and result meaning thus constituting counterexamples to the MRC. Finally, I will have a close look at the three verbs in (63)d to check further whether they violate the lexical constraint prescribed by the MRC.

(63) Manner-of-motion verbs

    a. 跳 tiào "jump", 滚 gǔn "roll", 爬 pá "climb",

       奔 bēn "run quickly", 转 zhuǎn "turn", 跨 kuà "stride",

       冲 chōng "dash", 溜 līu "slide/sneak", 拐 guǎi "turn",

       追 zhuī "chase"

    b. 钻 zuān "squeeze", 退 tuì "recede", 落 luò "fall",

       陷 xiàn "sink", 穿 chuān "pass through", 越 yuè "pass over"

c. 登 dēng "mount", 掉 diào "fall"

d. 跑 pǎo "run", 走 zǒu "walk", 飞 fēi "fly"

There is no controversy over the ontological type of verbs in (63)a, since encoding the obvious and clear manner of motion they exhibit typical grammatical behaviors of manner verbs. They are atelic activity verbs and compatible with durative time adverbial, as can be seen in (64)a. They do not entail the direction of motion, so they are compatible with varied path information. The sentence in (64)b shows that the manner verb 爬 pá "climb" specifies no direction, so it is compatible with various directions 上 shàng "ascend", 下 xià "descend," 进 jìn "enter" and 出 chū "exit". In contrast with directed motion verbs, these manner verbs allow unsubcategorized objects. As can be seen in (64)c, it is completely acceptable for the verb 跳 tiào "jump" to take the unsubcategorized object 一头汗 yì tóu hàn "his head covered with sweat" as its complement.

(64) a. 他   爬   了   三十   分钟。

tā   pá   le   sānshí   fēnzhōng

he   climb   ASP   thirty   minute

"He climbed for thirty minutes."

b. 孩子   们   爬   上   爬   下，   爬   进   爬   出，

háizi   men   pá   shàng   pá   xià   pá   jìn   pá   chū

child   PL   climb ascend climb descend climb enter climb exit

在   树屋   玩   了   一   天。

zài   shùwū   wán   le   yì   tiān

at   tree house   play   ASP   one   day

"Climbing up and down, and in and out, children played at the tree house all day long."

c. 他   跳   了   一   头   汗。

tā   tiào   le   yì   tóu   hàn

he   jump   ASP   one   head   sweat

"He   jumped   (continuously)   making   his   head   covered   with   sweat."

Chen and Guo (2009) are correct in classifying the verbs in (63)a as manner verbs because they all lexicalize non-scalar changes and exhibit grammatical behaviors typical to manner verbs. The controversial verbs in (63)b, (63)c and (63)d will be discussed in the following sections.

3.3.2   Controversies over Classification of Some Motion Verbs

Though Chen and Guo (2009) also classify all the verbs in group (63)b as manner verbs, other scholars categorize some of them as directed motion verbs. For example, Lamarre (2008) classifies 钻 zuān "squeeze" and 穿 chuān "pass through" as a path verb. Lin (2011) classifies 落 luò "fall", 退 tuì "recede" and 越 yuè "pass over" as path verbs. Upon the controversies, I will reexamine the grammatical behaviors of these verbs so as to clarify the ontological category of these verbs. With the criteria for determining manner and result verbs discussed above, I suggest that Chen and Guo are correct in classifying the verb 钻 zuān "squeeze" as a manner verb, but they cannot be correct to regard all the other verbs in (63)b as manner verbs too. Rather I believe the other verbs 穿 chuān "pass through", 落 luò "fall", 退 tuì "recede" and 越 yuè "pass over" are actually path verbs, in line with Lamarre (2008) and Lin (2011).

First, the grammatical behaviors of the verb 钻 zuān "squeeze" conform to those of manner verbs, so it is correct to classify it as a manner verb. As seen in (65)a, 钻 zuān "squeeze" does not pose any constraint on the path information it may co-occur with, so it reveals that the verb itself does not lexicalize the path at all. In addition, it also allows to be followed by unsubcategorized objects and by elements indicating distinct scalar changes. In (65)b, 钻 zuān "squeeze" takes 破头 pò tóu "break head" as a second predicate to indicate a distinct scalar change. Aspectually it also conforms to the property of manner verbs, since it also shows the atelic aspectual feature of manner verbs. In (65)c, it is compatible with durative time adverbial 一直 yīzhí "continuously".

(65) a. 钻　　　　进/出/上/下/回
zuān　　　jìn/chū/shàng/xià/huí
squeeze enter/exit/ascend/descend/return
"squeeze in/out/up/down/back"

b. 他 们 钻 破 头 也 要 挤 进 去。
tā men zuān pò tóu yě yào jǐ jìn qù
he PL squeeze broke head also will squeeze enter go
"They wanted to squeeze in even at the cost of getting their
heads broken."

c. 蚯蚓 一直 往 土 里 钻。
qiūyǐn yìzhí wǎng tǔ lǐ zuān
earthworm continuously toward earth inside squeeze
"The earthworm continuously squeezes into the earth."

Judged from these tests, the verb 钻 zuān "squeeze" is undoubtedly a manner
verb. Lamarre (2008) takes it as a path verb probably because she thinks it entails a
path of getting into some space, but the test in (65)a tells us that it is not true, since
it is compatible with varied directions of motion.

Then it is left to prove the other verbs in (63)b are all path verbs. The following
tests demonstrate that it is indeed the case. Conforming to the most obvious hallmark
of path verbs, these verbs encode the inherent direction of motion as their lexical
entailments, which cannot be violated. As illustrated in example (66)a, 落 luò "fall"
and 陷 xiàn "sink" are only compatible with the downward direction 下 xià "descend",
which is just the direction encoded in the verb, but incompatible with the upward
direction 上 shàng "ascend", which violates their lexicalized direction. The same is
true for 退 tuì "recede". As it lexicalizes a backward direction of motion, it is
incompatible with the adverbial phrase indicating a forward direction 向前 xiàng

qián "toward forward", as illustrated by the contrast in (66)c and (66)d. Besides, these verbs do not allow phrases denoting other scales to be their complements. For instance, it is possible that a kite breaks its wings as a result of falling from sky, but as seen in (67)a the verb 落 luò "fall" cannot be followed by the phrase 断了翅膀 duàn le chìbǎng "break ASP wings". Similarly, as a result of receding, the enemy may lose their morale, but it is unacceptable to have the phrase 丢了士气 diū le shìqì "lose ASP morale" follow the verb 退 tuì "recede", as illustrated in (67)b.

(66) a. 落/陷　　　下　　　去
　　　　luò/xiàn　xià　　qù
　　　　fall/sink　descend　go
　　　　"fall/sink" (Away from the speaker)

　　　b. *落/陷　　　上　　　去
　　　　luò/xiàn　shàng　qù
　　　　fall/sink　ascend　go
　　　　"#fall/sink upward" (Intended meaning)

　　　c. 向　　　后　　　退
　　　　xiàng　hòu　tuì
　　　　toward　back　recede
　　　　"recede backward"

　　　d. *向　　　前　　　退
　　　　xiàng　qián　tuì
　　　　toward　front　recede
　　　　"#recede forward"

(67) a. *风筝　　　落　　断　　了　　翅膀。
　　　　fēngzheng　luò　duàn　le　chìbǎng
　　　　kite　　　　fall　broken　ASP　wing
　　　　"#The kite fell its wings broken."

b. *敌人　　退　　丢　　了　　士气。

dírén　　tuì　　diū　　le　　shìqì

enemy　　recede　　lose　　ASP　　morale

"#The enemy lost their morale as a result of their receding."

Contrastively, these verbs do not encode the manner of motion, so they are compatible with various manners. For example, the verb 落 luò "fall" can be combined with various manners of motion such as 滴 dī "drip", 滑 huá "slide" or 漂 piāo "float" to describe what manner the falling is carried out, as can be seen in (68)a. In (68)b, the verb 退 tuì "recede" can also be modified by different manners of motion such as walking, running and clambering.

(68) a. 滴/滑/飘　　　落　　下　　　来

dī/huá/piāo　　luò　xià　　lái

drip/slide/float　fall　descend　come

"fall down towards the deictic center in a dripping/sliding/ floating manner"

b. 走/跑/爬　　　着　　往　　后　　　退

zǒu/pǎo/pá　　zhe　　wǎng　hòu　　tuì

zou/run/clamber　DUR　toward　backward　recede

"to recede backward by walking/running/clambering"

The verbs 穿 chuān "pass through" and 越 yuè "pass over" are different from the three verbs discussed above because they are rarely used as free morphemes. Scholars (e.g. Packard, 2000; Hsiao, 2009) note that not all monomorphemic verbs are free morphemes in Mandarin. Many monosyllabic roots are bound up and must combine with another free/bound root word to form disyllabic verbs. When used as motion verbs, 穿 chuān "pass through" and 越 yuè "pass over" fall into this type, but in spite of their morphosyntactic property as bound morphemes, I consider them as path roots because they do show grammatical properties of path verbs.

On the one hand, when used as motion verbs, they can only be followed by path information which is compatible to their lexicalized directions such as 过 guò "pass" in 穿/越过 chuān/yuè guò "pass through/over", but not with other verbs indicating contradictory path information such as 下 xià "descend" in *穿/越下 chuān/yuè xià "pass downward". On the other hand, they are compatible with varied cause or manner information. As shown in (69), 穿 chuān "pass through" is compatible with different actions such as 打 dǎ "beat" and 戳 chuō "poke". Likewise, 越 yuè "pass over" also appears with different manner verbs such as 飞 fēi "fly" and 跨 kuà "stride".

(69) a. 打/击/戳   穿

dǎ/jī/chuō   chuān

beat/strike/poke   pass.through

"beat/strike/poke a way through"

b. 飞/跨   越

fēi/kuà   yuè

fly/stride   pass.over

"fly/stride over"

Though there are controversies over the ontological categorization of verbs in (63)b, with clear criteria these verbs can be classified in a consistent way. The verb 钻 zuān "squeeze" is a manner verb, and the other verbs 退 tuì "recede", 落 luò "fall", 陷 xiàn "sink", 穿 chuān "pass through", and 越 yuè "pass over" are actually path verbs.

3.3.3 Potential Counterexample Verbs

The two verbs in group (63)c 掉 diào "fall" and 登 dēng "mount" are also classified as manner-of-motion verbs by Chen and Guo (2009), but scholars such as Ma (2008), Hsiao (2009) and Shi and Wu (2014) propose that these two verbs encode both manner and path meaning components. If their claim is true, these two verbs will constitute counterexamples to the MRC and thus undermine the validity of the MRC. Therefore, it is essential to analyze the lexicalized meaning and grammatical behaviors of these verbs so as to clarify their categorization. A closer look at the grammatical behaviors reveals that these verbs actually only encode the path information and they are path verbs.

Hsiao (2009) argues that the verb 掉 diào "fall" lexicalizes both a path in accordance with the direction of the gravity and the force of gravity which should be regarded as the manner property of the verb. However, as discussed in Section 3.2, the concept of force of gravity is in fact a reference for the direction of motion, so it cannot be regarded as a lexicalized manner in the verb. This point is attested in its grammatical behaviors. An example provided by Lin (2011) is concerning the situation where the verb 掉 diào "fall" is used to describe a situation where a truck falls off a bridge. As she explains, the engine of the truck may be broken and the wheels may be lost, but these results are not compatible with the path of falling, so 掉 diào "fall" does not allow the phrases expressing these results to be followed as its complements, as shown in (70).

(70) a. *货车　　　掉坏　　　　　发动机了。

huòchē　　diào huài　　　fādòngjī le

truck　　　fall-be.broken　　engine ASP

"The engine of the truck was broken as a result of the falling of the truck."(Intended meaning)

b. *货车　　掉 丢 轮子了。

huòchē　　diàodiū　lúnzi le

truck　　　fall-lose　wheel ASP

"The truck lost its wheels as a result of its falling." (Intended meaning)

(Cited in Lin, 2011)

Shi and Wu (2014) make similar proposal that the verb 登 dēng "mount" encodes not merely manner but also the path information. These authors point out that in example (71)a 登 dēng "mount", on the one hand, is the main verb of the directional compound conveying the manner of the motion, but on the other hand, since except for the upward direction the verb is not compatible with all the other directional complements, as illustrated in (71)b, the verb also lexicalizes the upward movement. However, if we check the grammatical behaviors of the verb, we can determine 登 dēng "mount" is a directed motion verb, in which no manner is lexicalized.

(71) a. 接着　　我　登　　上　　　十米　　高台。
　　　　jiēzhe　wǒ　dēng　shàng　shímǐ　gāotái
　　　　then　　I　　mount　ascend　ten-meter　platform
　　　　"Then I went up to the ten-meter platform."

(Shi & Wu, 2014)

　　b. *登　　　下/进/出
　　　　dēng　　xià/jìn/chū
　　　　mount　descend/enter/exit
　　　　"#mount down/in/out" (Intended meaning)

Shi and Wu are correct in claiming that 登 dēng "mount" lexicalizes the upward direction of motion, since the example (71)b shows that the upward direction cannot be violated. However, probably judging the manner component of the verb only based on intuition, they do not specify what manner 登 dēng "mount" encodes exactly. Based on a careful study of the actual uses of the verb in the CCL corpus[①], I observe that there is no manner encoded in the verb and 登 dēng "mount" is only a path verb. The data in the CCL corpus show that one of the prototypical activities the verb involves is 登山 dēng shān "mount mountain". It

---

[①] The CCL corpus is developed by Center for Chinese Linguistics at Peking University and it is available online http://ccl.pku.edu.cn:8080/ccl_corpus/.

can be predicted that if 登 dēng "mount" specifies the manner of motion, some patterns of movements of legs or hands must be involved. However, there are a dozen of examples describing the event of 登山 dēng shān "mount mountain" in a cable car, in which no manner can be possibly involved as people just sit in the cable car and go up to the top of the mountain with the help of engine power of the car, as illustrated in (72).

(72) 我们　　经过　　两　　　个　小时　　的　　　漫长
　　　wǒmen jīngguò liǎng　gè xiǎoshí de　　màncháng
　　　I PL　 through two　　CL hour　　NOM　 long
　　　等待　　后　　才　　得以　乘　　　缆车　　登　　上
　　　děngdài hòu　 cái　déyǐ chéng lǎnchē　dēng shàng
　　　wait　　after only can　take　 cable.car mount ascend
　　　天子　　山。
　　　Tiānzǐ　shān
　　　Tianzi　Mountain
"After two hours' long waiting we went up to the top of Tianzi Mountain in a cable car."

(CCL Corpus)

The manner sense is probably a derived pragmatic inference from the activity the verb is conventionally associated with, since mountain climbing is generally regarded as involving deliberate effort and certain manners such as clambering with limbs. Nevertheless, a pragmatic sense is different from a lexical meaning, because it is derived from the supporting contexts or encyclopedic knowledge and it is not constant across contexts. For example, when the verb 登 dēng "mount" takes other arguments such as 陆 lù "land" and 台 tái "stage/platform", no specific manner is entailed and the only sense the verb describes is "go up to a higher place from a lower place", as illustrated in (73). Thus it can be seen that the verb 登 dēng "mount" is only a path verb.

(73) a. 台风　每　年　夏天　　从　这 个 岛　上　　登陆。

　　　 táifēng měi nián xiàtiān cóng zhè gè dǎo shàng dēnglù

　　　 typhoon every year summer from this CL island LOC　land

　　　 "Every summer typhoons mount the land from this island."

　 b. 她　六　岁　开始　登台　　　演出。

　　　 tā liù suì kāishǐ dēngtái　yǎnchū

　　　 she six age start mount stage perform

　　　 "She went up to the stage performing at six."

In summary, the actual uses of the verb 掉 diào "fall" and 登 dēng "mount" show they only lexicalize the direction of the motion, and the manner information is inferred from the contexts but not entailed. Thus they cannot be counterexamples to the MRC.

3.3.4 Neglected Motion Verbs in Previous Studies

The three verbs 走 zǒu "walk", 跑 pǎo "run" and 飞 fēi "fly" listed in (63)d are all categorized as manner-of-motion verbs in previous studies but I observe that they lexicalize the directed motion when used in some constructions. In addition, when we check their actual uses, they also pose a problem for the tests for manner verbs: though in their basic uses they can pass the tests for manner-of-motion verbs, in some other cases their syntactic distributions just contradict the property of manner-of-motion verbs. For example, as prototypical manner-of-motion verbs, they are not expected to co-occur with verbs which express distinct manner information, since verbs specifying different manners should not be compatible. Nevertheless, as illustrated in (74), in their actual uses they can co-occur with verbs specifying distinct manners.

(74) a. 气球　　飘　走　了。

　　　 qìqiú piāo zǒu le

　　　 balloon float-walk ASP

"The balloon flew away."

b. 皮球　　滚　　跑　　了。

píqiú　　gǔn　pǎo　　le

rubber　ball　roll-run　ASP

"The rubber ball rolled away."

c. 鞋子　被　　踢　飞　了。

xiézǐ　bèi　　tī　fēi　le

shoe　PASS　kick-fly　ASP

"The shoe was kicked away."

In (74)a 走 zǒu "walk" co-occurs with another manner verb 漂 piāo "float", in (74)b 跑 pǎo "run" also co-occurs with another manner verb 滚 gǔn "roll" and in (74)c 飞 fēi "fly" follows another manner verb 踢 tī "kick".

Moreover, the inconsistent grammatical behaviors of the three verbs can also be attested when they are used in another construction, i.e. the three verbs can be found in subject inversion constructions, as shown in (75). In Chinese, without getting combined with other path indicating elements, manner-of-motion verbs generally cannot be used in subject inversion constructions (Yuan, 1999), but the three verbs can be used in this way. More importantly, they share this property with prototypical path verbs such as 来 lái "come" and 去 qù "go" in (76), but not with other manner-of-motion verbs such as 跳 tiào "jump" and 爬 pá "crawl" in (77).

(75) a. 走　了　一　个　学生。

zǒu　le　yī　gè　xuéshēng.

walk　ASP　one　CL　student

"A student left."

b. 飞　了　一　只　鸽子。

fēi　le　yī　zhī　gēzi

fly   ASP   one   CL   pigeon

"A pigeon flew away."

(76) a. 来　　了　　一　　个　　职员。

　　　lái　　le　　yī　　gè　　zhíyuán

　　　come   ASP   one   CL   employee

　　　"Here came an employee."

　　b. 去　　了　　一　　个　　老师。

　　　qù　　le　　yī　　gè　　lǎoshī

　　　go   ASP   one   CL   teacher

　　　"There went a teacher."

(77) a. *跳　　了　　一　　个　　小孩。

　　　tiào　　le　　yī　　gè　　xiǎohái

　　　jump   ASP   one   CL   child

　　　"A child jumped." (Intended meaning)

　　b. *爬　　了　　一　　条　　毛毛虫。

　　　pá　　le　　yī　　tiáo　　máomáochóng

　　　crawl   ASP   one   CL   caterpillar

　　　"A caterpillar crawled." (Intended meaning)

The inconsistent grammatical behaviors of these verbs illustrated above force us to ask whether they can indeed encode both the manner and direction of motion together and then constitute counterexamples to the MRC.

Though the validity of the MRC ultimately rests on the lack of counterexample verbs which encode both manner and result, it is also possible to argue for the hypothesis by inspecting the obvious polysemous verbs which can possibly lexicalize either result or manner, but there is never a single use of the verb which entails both meaning components together. Though Rappaport Hovav and Levin

(1998) take the position that languages maintain minimal number of polysemous verbs, they do admit some verbs indeed have two distinct senses with one encoding manner the other result. For instance, in arguing against the purported counterexamples to the MRC, Levin and Rappaport Hovav (2013) examine different uses of the English verb climb and observe that though in its typical uses the basic meaning of climb is manner of motion, i.e. "force exertion against gravity" (Levin, Rappaport Hovav, 2013), when used with "abstract themes", the verb indeed encode an upward direction and in these cases climb can be regarded as a result verb. More essentially, when it lexicalizes the direction of motion, as noted by Levin and Rappaport Hovav, the manner meaning component is dropped.

I suggest that the three motion verbs 走 zǒu "walk", 跑 pǎo "run" and 飞 fēi "fly" fall into the same category as the English verb climb: in their typical uses, they lexicalize the manner of motion and conform to the hallmarks of manner verbs; however, when they are used as the second verb in a directional verbal compound following another verb expressing distinct manner information or in a subject inversion construction, they encode the direction of motion and behave as result verbs. More importantly, they lose their manner meaning when they are used as result verbs. In the following section, applying the criteria for determining manner or result verbs, I will illustrate the specific uses of these three verbs to verify the claim.

3.3.4.1 走 zǒu "walk", 跑 pǎo "run" and 飞 fēi "fly" Used as Manner-of-Motion Verbs

In their basic uses, there is no doubt that the three verbs show hallmarks of manner verbs. As they lexicalize non-scalar changes, they are necessarily atelic and compatible with durative time adverbial. As illustrated in (78)a, 走 zǒu "walk" is compatible with durative time adverbial 三个小时 sān gè xiǎo shí "three hours". In (78)b 飞 fēi "fly" can be used with durative time adverbial 三天 sān tiān "three days".

(78) a. 他 走 了 三 个 小时。

　　　 tā zǒu le sān gè xiǎo shí

　　　 he walk ASP three CL hour

　　　 "He walked for three hours."

b. 小　鸟　飞　了　三天。

xiǎo　niǎo　fēi　le　sān tiān

little　bird　fly　ASP　three days

"The little bird flew for three days."

Since they do not entail any direction or result information, they can take varied result and path phrases as their complements. As illustrated in (79)a, 跑 pǎo "run" is compatible with both upward and downward directions. It is also shown that in (79)b 飞 fēi "fly" can take 断 duàn "break (wings)" and in (79)c 跑 pǎo "run" can take 丢鞋 dīu xié "lose shoes" as their resultant complements respectively.

(79) a. 战士们　　　每　天　跑　上　跑　下。

zhànshì men　měi　tiān　pǎo shàng pǎo xià

soldier　PL　every day　run-ascend-run-descend

"Soldiers run up and down every day."

b. 他们　的　翅膀　都　快　飞　断　了。

tā mén de　chì bǎng dōu kuài fēi duàn le

they-PL POSS wings　almost　fly-break ASP

"They (pigeons) almost broke their wings as a result of flying (continuously)."

c. 他　跑　丢　鞋子　了。

tā　pǎo diū　xiézi　le

he　run-lose　shoe　ASP

"He lost his shoes as a result of running."

It can be seen that in their basic uses the lexicalized meaning and grammatical behaviors of the three verbs conform to the property of manner-of-motion verbs.

They are compatible with varied directions of motion and resultative phrases. They also show atelic aspectual features prototypical to manner verbs.

3.3.4.2 走 zǒu "walk", 跑 pǎo "run" and 飞 fēi "fly" Used as Directed Motion Verbs

As mentioned in previous sections, the three verbs can be found to exhibit grammatical behaviors distinct from manner-of-motion verbs, since they can be used in subject inversion constructions and they can also follow another manner-of-motion verb to form a verbal compound without contradiction. Focusing on the two specific cases, this section uses a series of syntactic and semantic tests to check what lexical meaning they actually encode and to clarify their ontological status.

First, I will show that when the three motion verbs are used in subject inversion constructions they only encode directed motion and their manner-of-motion sense is dropped out. In Chinese, it is generally accepted by scholars (Li, 1990; Yu, 1995) that verbs which are used with perfective aspectual markers in subject inversion constructions are prototypical unaccusative verbs. These verbs generally describe a non-volitional change-of-state/location of the theme. As illustrated in (80)a, the verb 死 sǐ "die" describing a non-volitional change-of-state is an unaccusative verb, so it can be used in the subject inversion construction. Nevertheless, in (80)b 唱 chàng "sing" expressing a volitional action is an unergative verb, so it cannot be used in the construction.

(80) a. 死　了　一　个　人。
　　　sǐ　le　yī　gè　rén
　　　die ASP one CL person
　　　"A person died."

　　b. *唱　了　一　个　人。
　　　chàng le　yī　gè rén
　　　sing　ASP one CL person
　　　"A person sang." (Intended meaning)

Though generally manner-of-motion verbs are regarded as unergative verbs which, without getting combined with other path morphemes, cannot enter the subject inversion construction, the three verbs can be used in the construction, as shown in the example sentence of (75)a. With regard to these cases, I suggest that these verbs entail only the directed motion as "depart from the reference object". Crucially as is shown by their grammatical properties in this construction, they lose their manner meaning components. First, when they are used in this construction, they lose the atelic aspectual feature of manner verbs and encode punctual and telic changes. The examples in (81) show that they are not compatible with durative aspectual marker 着 zhe.

(81) *a. 走　着　一　个　学生。

      zǒu　zhe　yī　gè　xuéshēng

      walk　DUR　one　CL　student

      "A student is leaving." (Intended meaning)

   *b. 跑　着　一　个　犯人。

      pǎo　zhe　yī　gè　fànrén

      run　DUR　one　CL　prisoner

      "A prisoner is running away." (Intended meaning)

   *c. 飞　着　一　只　鸽子。

      fēi　zhe　yī　zhī　gēzi

      fly　DUR　one　CL　pigeon

      "A pigeon is flying away." (Intended meaning)

In addition, when the three verbs are used in subject inversion constructions they cannot be modified by action-oriented manner adverbials, as shown in (82). This also indicates that the manner-of-motion sense of the verbs is dropped out and they only encode the directed motion sense.

(82) *a. 迅速　　地　　走　了　一　个　学生。

　　　xùnsù　de　zǒu　le　yí　gè　xuésheng

　　　swiftly　ADV　walk　ASP　one　CL　student

　　　"A student left swiftly." (Intended meaning)

　　*b. 拼命　　　地　　跑　了　一　个　　犯人。

　　　pīnmìng　de　pǎo　le　yí　gè　fànrén

　　　desperately　ADV　run　ASP　one　CL　prisoner

　　　"A prisoner ran away desperately." (Intended meaning)

　　*c. 敏捷　　地　　飞　了　一　只　鸽子。

　　　mǐnjié　de　fēi　le　yì　zhī　gēzi

　　　nimbly　ADV　fly　ASP　one　CL　pigeon

　　　"A pigeon flew away nimbly." (Intended meaning)

It can be predicted that if the verb 走 zǒu "walk" also encodes the manner of motion, judged from its lexical semantics, a motion carried out in a walking manner by a student should be modified by the adverb 迅速地 xùnsù de "swiftly". Similarly, it is natural that a prisoner runs desperately and a pigeon flies nimbly. However, the sentences in (82) indicate that the three verbs cannot be modified by corresponding action-oriented adverbs 迅速地 xùnsù de "swiftly", 拼命地 pīnmìng de "desperately" and 敏捷地 mǐnjié de "nimbly". Thus it shows that used in subject inversion constructions, the manner sense of the three verbs has been dropped out, and they only encode the directed motion sense.

Another case that the three verbs show distinct grammatical behaviors from manner-of-motion verbs is when they follow another verb to form verbal compounds, as shown in (74). Based on Chinese morphology when two verbs co-occur to form a verbal compound there are mainly three types of possible relationship between the two component verbs: coordination, modification, and resultative relation (Packard, 2000). The grammatical behaviors of these verbal compounds in (74) show that they are actually resultative verbal compounds ruling out the other two possibilities. On the one hand, the two component verbs express distinct manners which are incompatible to each other and thus they cannot hold coordinating relation. On the other hand, the two component verbs do not hold modifying relation either, since for this kind of verbal compounds in which the first verb (V1) functions as an adverbial to further specify the action denoted by the second verb (V2) (e.g. 飞奔 fēi-bēn "fly-run" "to run (quickly) like flying") it is not possible to add the negation marker bù in between to form potential constructions (e.g. *飞不奔 fēi-bù-bēn "fly-NEG-run" "#not be able to run by flying"). However the verbal compounds in (74) can do so, as shown in (83), which is just one of the properties shared by resultative verbal compounds in Chinese. Thus it is clear that the component verbs in (74) hold resultative relation.

(83) 漂   不   走

     piāo bù   zǒu

     float-NEG-walk

     "not be able to float away"

As for motion events, the two juxtaposing verbs form a directional verbal compound (DVC), a subtype of resultative verbal compounds in which V1 usually specifies the manner or cause of the motion and V2 expresses the direction of motion. In the case of verbal compounds in (74), the verbs holding V1 position 飘 piāo "float", 滚 gǔn "roll" and 踢 tī "kick" specify the manner of motion, and the verbs occupying the V2 position 走 zǒu "walk", 跑 pǎo "run" and 飞 fēi "fly" describe the direction of the motion.

This analysis is supported by the contrastive semantic entailments of example sentences in (84) and (85). As shown in (84), the manner-of-motion verbs 飘 piāo "float", 滚 gǔn "roll" and 踢 tī "kick" do not entail displacement of the theme. In the sentence of (84)a, 飘 piāo "float" describes that small flags were floating on the top of the flag pole where flags were tied and thus no displacement is possible. Similarly, in (84)b 滚 gǔn "roll" and 踢 tī "kick" describe actions in place, so there is no displacement either.

(84) a. 旗杆　　　上　　飘　　着　　小旗。

qígān　　　shàng　piāo　zhe　　xiǎo qí

flagpole　LOC　　float　IMP　small flag

"Small flags were floating on the top of the flag pole."

b. 他在　原地　　　　滚/踢。

tā zài　yuándì　　　gǔn/tī

he at　original place　kick/roll

"He rolled/kicked in place."

Nonetheless, when 走 zǒu "walk", 跑 pǎo "run" and 飞 fēi "fly" are added following these verbs to form verbal compounds, displacement of the theme as "departing from a reference object" is entailed. In (85)a 飘走 piāo zǒu "float-walk" entails that the flags floated away and they were not on the top of the flag pole anymore. Similarly, the verbal compounds 滚跑 gǔn pǎo "roll-run" and 踢飞 tī fēi "kick-fly" also entail the themes have left the deictic object, as illustrated in (85)b and (85)c.

(85) a. 小旗　飘　走　　　　了,* 但 它 还 在 旗杆　　上。

xiǎoqí piāo zǒu　　　le　dàn tā hái zài qígān　shàng

small　flag float-walk ASP but it still at flagpole LOC

"Flag floated away, #but it was still on the top of the flag pole."

b. 皮球　　　滚跑　　了,*但　它　还　在　　原地。

píqiú　　　gǔn pǎo le　dàn tā hái zài　yuándì

rubber ball roll-run ASP but　it still at　original place

"The rubber ball rolled away, #but it still stayed at its original place."

　　c. 鞋子　被　　踢飞　了，*但　鞋子　还　在　　脚　上。

　　　 xiézi　bèi　　tī fēi　le　　dàn xiézi　hái　zài　jiǎo　shàng

　　　 shoe PASS kick-fly ASP　but shoe still　at　　foot LOC

　　　 "The shoe was kicked off, #but it was still on the foot."

　　Distinct lexical entailments can also be attested by looking at the aspectual features of these DVCs. As illustrated in (86), when the three verbs are used as V2 to form DVCs, these DVCs are incompatible with the progressive aspectual marker 正在 zhèngzài and durative aspectual marker 着 zhe. This indicates that though all the component verbs of these DVCs are typically atelic, these DVCs have lost their atelic aspectual features and become telic.

　　(86) a. *气球　　　正在　　　　飘　走　着。

　　　　　 qìqiú　　　zhèngzài piāo zǒu　zhe

　　　　　 balloon PROG　　　 float-walk DUR

　　　　　 "The balloon is floating away." (Intended meaning)

　　　　 b. *皮球　　　　正在　　　滚　跑　着。

　　　　　 pí qiú　　　 zhèngzài gǔn pǎo　zhe

　　　　　 rubber ball PROG　　　 roll-run DUR

　　　　　 "The rubber ball is rolling away." (Intended meaning)

　　　　 c. *鞋子　　正在　　　　被　踢　飞　着。

　　　　　 xiézi　zhèngzài bèi　　tī　fēi　zhe

　　　　　 shoe PROG　　　PASS kick-fly DUR

　　　　　 "The shoe is being kicked off." (Intended meaning)

　　The change of aspectual features can also be supported by the contrastive readings of the post-verbal adverbial "for X time" when it co-occurs with only the manner verbs in V1 position or with the DVCs. To be specific, as in (87) when the manner verbs holding V1 position co-occur with a post-verbal adverbial "for X time", there is only an atelic process reading.

(87) a. 气球　　飘　　了　　一　　小时　　了。

　　　　qìqiú　　piāo　le　　yī　　xiǎoshí　le

　　　　balloon　float　ASP　one　hour　　CRS

　　　　"The balloon has floated for an hour."

b. 皮球　　　滚　了　　一　　分钟　　　了。

　　píqiú　　　gǔn　le　　yī　　fēnzhōng le

　　rubber ball　roll　ASP　one　minute　　CRS

　　"The rubber ball has rolled for a minute."

c. 鞋子　被　踢　　了　　一　　分钟　　　了。

　　xiézi　bèi　tī　　le　　yī　　fēnzhōng le

　　shoe　PASS　kick　ASP　one　minute　　CRS

　　"The shoe has been kicked for a minute."

In contrast, when the post-verbal adverbial "for X time" co-occurs with the DVCs, the time period indicated by the adverbial only has a "after X time" reading which specifies the length of time that the result state of "depart from the reference object" holds, as seen in (88). This further indicates that the DVC as a whole describes a two-point scalar change.

(88) a. 气球　　飘　走　了　　一　　小时　　了。

　　　　qìqiú　　piāo zǒu　le　　yī　　xiǎoshí　le

　　　　balloon　float-walk　ASP　one　hour　　CRS

　　　　"It had been an hour since the balloon floated away."

b. 皮球　　　滚　跑　了　一　　分钟　　　了。

　　píqiú　　　gǔn pǎo　le　yī　　fēnzhōng　le

　　rubber ball　roll-run　ASP　one　minute　　CRS

"It had been a minute since the rubber ball rolled away."

c. 鞋子　被　　踢 飞 了　一　分钟　　　了。

　　xiézi　bèi　　tī　fēi　le　yī　fēnzhōng　le

　　shoe　PASS　kick-fly ASP one minute　CRS

"It had been a minute since the shoe was kicked off."

Thus it is safe to believe that the change of the aspectual feature from atelic to telic is attributed to the three verbs holding V2 position and these verbs have dropped their manner sense. The puzzling problem that the three verbs violate the linguistic tests for manner-of-motion verbs is also clear now. In these cases, the three verbs do not encode the manner of motion at all, and instead they only express the direction of the motion. That's why they can co-occur with another manner-of-motion verb without contradiction.

Summarizing, when the three prototypical manner-of-motion verbs exhibit different grammatical behaviors, they also lexicalize distinct meaning components. To be specific, when used in subject inversion constructions and when they follow another manner-of-motion verb to form a DVC, they lose their manner sense and lexicalize only the sense of directed motion.

3.3.4.3 Two Distinct Senses of 走 zǒu "walk", 跑 pǎo "run" and 飞 fēi "fly" in Complementary Distribution

Some may argue the directed motion sense of the three motion verbs may not be the lexical entailment of the verb, and it may be derived from the meaning of the construction they are found in or from other pragmatic factors. In Section 3.3.4.2 the directed motion sense of the three verbs has been examined based on two typical constructions in Chinese, so it is natural to assume that the directed motion sense is derived from the constructions. In addition, Levin et al. (2009) argue that cross-linguistically manner-of-motion verbs share the same type of verb roots: they all specify only the manner of motion and the sense of directed motion arise from pragmatic factors. However, I suggest neither case is true for the three motion verbs in Chinese. The directed motion sense is not derived from other elements of the sentence and it is indeed the lexicalized meaning in the verbs because the three verbs can have a directed motion reading even though they are not used in the two constructions and without pragmatic support from contexts. For example, as illustrated in (89), without any contextual support the simple sentence with the verb 走 zǒu "walk" as its only verb is ambiguous. It has two possible interpretations: either "I am capable of walking" or "I can leave". Therefore, it can be seen that the directed motion sense is not derived from the two constructions; rather it is because the three verbs can possibly lexicalize the directed motion so that they can enter the two constructions.

(89) 我　能　　走　了。

　　 wǒ　néng　zǒu　le

　　 I　can　walk　ASP

　　 a. "I am capable of walking."

　　 b. "I can leave."

Interestingly, with the former reading "I am capable of walking" the verb 走 zǒu "walk" only encodes the manner of motion and for the latter reading "I can leave" the verb only lexicalizes the directed motion as "depart from a reference object". Though the verb can potentially encode both manner and direction of motion, the sentence never entails "I can leave by walking". As illustrated in (90), when used in the directed motion sense, 走 zǒu "walk" is compatible with varied ways of moving such as 坐船 zuò chuán "by boat" and 坐火车 zuò huǒchē "by train". In contrast, when it is used in the manner sense, it is compatible with varied directions of motion such as 出去 chūqù "exit in a direction away from the speaker" and 进来 jìnlái "enter in a direction coming near to the speaker".

(90) a. 我　能　坐　船/　坐　火车　　走。

　　　 wǒ　néng　zuò　chuán/　zuò　huǒchē　zǒu

　　　 I　can　sit　boat/　sit　train　walk

　　　 "I can leave by boat/by train."

b. 我　能　走　　出去/进来。

wǒ　néng　zǒu　　chūqù/jìnlái

I　can　walk　exit go/enter　come

"I can walk in/out."

In fact, it is just the direct evidence for the MRC as a general principle constraining how much meaning a verb can possibly lexicalize. Following Levin and Rappaport Hovav (2013), a lexicalized meaning component is one that is entailed across all uses of a verb. Though the three motion verbs can potentially lexicalize manner and result, but there is never a single use of the verb which entails both meaning components together. The MRC is a valid cross-linguistic principle that constrains the possible lexicalization patterns of the lexicon.

Focusing on three Chinese motion verbs 走 zǒu "walk", 跑 pǎo "run" and 飞 fēi "fly", this section investigates the lexicalization patterns of Chinese motion verbs. Different from the view of Levin et al. (2009) that manner-of-motion verbs only lexicalize the sense of manner, I suggest the three Chinese motion verbs can indeed lexicalize the direction of motion. However, they never encode the manner and direction of motion simultaneously and thus do not falsify the MRC. As far as the actual uses are concerned, the lexicalization patterns of these three verbs confirm the validity of MRC as a significant observation about how much meaning can be lexicalized in a verb.

3.4 Summary

This chapter investigates the cross-linguistic validity of the manner/result complementarity hypothesis in Modern Chinese motion verbs and finds that the lexical entailments and grammatical properties of Chinese motion verbs generally conform to the lexical constraint. Based on the manner-of-motion verbs and path verbs collected by Chen and Guo (2009), this chapter re-examines the lexicalization patterns of Chinese motion verbs with a particular focus on the classification of controversial verbs, potential counterexamples and polysemous verbs. Though scholars classify some manner-of-motion verbs differently, and put forward some counterexample verbs to the MRC, a careful study of them shows that the misclassification of verbs mainly results from the misconception of the notions of manner and result; the putative counterexample verbs which are claimed to lexicalize both path and manner are actually either manner or result verbs; while the polysemous verbs 走 zǒu "walk", 跑 pǎo "run" and 飞 fēi "fly" can lexicalize both manner and result meaning components, they never entail both simultaneously and thus do not falsify the MRC. This chapter reaffirms that the MRC is a significant lexical constraint on how much meaning a verb may lexicalize.

Chapter 4

The Manner/Result Complementarity in Old Chinese

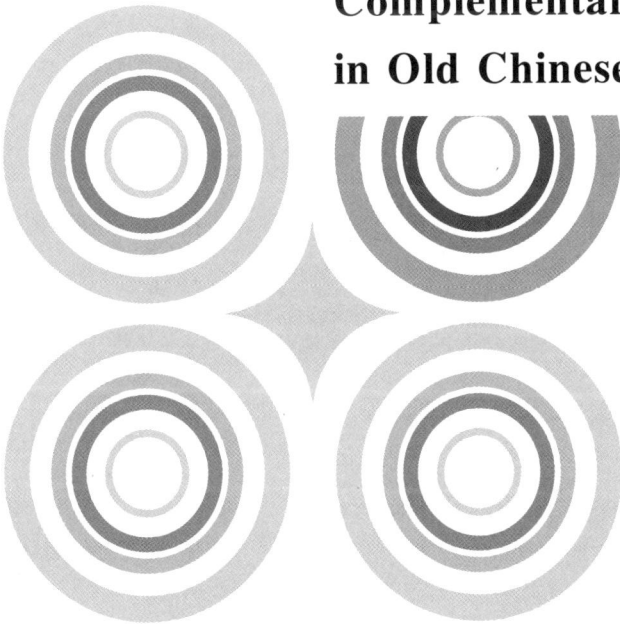

This chapter investigates the lexical semantics of motion verbs in Old Chinese to further reveal the possible lexicalization patterns of Chinese motion verbs and check the validity of the MRC. As a language with a long history, Chinese has undergone radical changes as to its phonological systems, lexical resources and morphosyntactic structures along its evolution from Old Chinese to Modern Chinese. Though many verbs in Old Chinese share the same graphic and phonetic representations with their counterparts in Modern Chinese, some of them have completely changed their grammatical category and thus cannot be used as verbs in Modern Chinese (e.g. 之 zhī "go", 适 shì "go", 如 rú "go"). While some other verbs still keep their verbal nature, the syntactic constructions in which they may appear are very different. For example, while the verb 走 zǒu "walk" in Modern Chinese cannot be immediately followed by locative nouns to indicate the goal of motion as can be seen in (91)a, it is completely acceptable in Old Chinese, as shown in (91).

(91) a. *走　　学校
　　　 zǒu　　xuéxiào
　　　 walk　school
　　　 "walk to school" (Intended meaning)

b. 奉　　君　　以　　　走　　固宫 (《左传》)
　 fèng　jūn　 yǐ　　 zǒu　Gùgōng
　 serve　king　CONJ　run　 Gu Palace
　 "serve the king to run to the Gu Palace"

As discussed in the previous chapter, motion verbs in Modern Chinese conform to the MRC, but it is not necessarily true in Old Chinese, as its lexicalization patterns of motion verbs are probably very different from Modern Chinese and it thus deserves independent investigation.

In addition, under Talmy's motion event framing theories, languages falling into different types, verb-framed or satellite-framed languages, tend to conflate either path or manner with motion in verbs respectively. However, according to Slobin (2004), the lexicalization of manner and path in motion verbs only exhibits a complementary distribution in satellite-framed languages but not in verb-framed languages. He points out that in spite of the major lexicalization patterns of conflating either manner or path with verbs across languages, some languages do have minor lexicalization patterns which conflate both manner and path with motion in verbs, and this kind of lexicalization patterns of motion verbs is in particular attested in some verb-framed languages, which, if true, would undermine the validity of the MRC. Thus it is necessary to check the lexicalization patterns of motion verbs in some verb-framed languages again. While Modern Chinese is generally regarded as a satellite-framed language, before undergoing a typological shift Old Chinese is considered as a verb-framed language. Thus from a typological perspective it is also significant to check the lexicalization patterns of motion verbs in Old Chinese. Researchers (Ma, 2008; Shi, Wu, 2014) investigating verbs in Old Chinese also cite some motion verbs such as 走 zǒu "run", 奔 bēn "rush" and 逃 táo "escape" which conflate both manner and path with motion. This chapter will have a close look at the lexicalization patterns of these verbs to reveal whether they constitute counterexamples to the MRC.

The organization of this part is as follows. Section 4.1 introduces some background information of Old Chinese concerning its general typological properties and motion events encoding. Section 4.2 explains the research methods and relevant data used in present studies. Section 4.3 provides a detailed discussion of the lexicalization patterns of motion verbs in Old Chinese. Section 4.4 summarizes the study of lexicalization patterns of motion verbs in Old Chinese.

4.1 Background of Old Chinese

4.1.1 Key Typological Characteristics of Old Chinese

The history of the Chinese language is featured by an evolution from monosyllabic to disyllabic words (e.g. Wang, 1980; Guo, 1986). In Modern Chinese, disyllabic words count most part of the lexicon, but in Old Chinese most words are believed to be monosyllabic. In Old Chinese period, only about 20% of the lexicon is disyllabic (Guo, 1997). Li (2007) counts the monosyllables and disyllables in two works composed in Old Chinese period, 《论语》 and 《孟子》, indicating that disyllabic words only take up about 22% of the whole lexicon. The monosyllabic feature of Old Chinese verbs can be best attested by the contrast between their morphological forms in Old Chinese and their corresponding Modern Chinese translation in (92).

    (92) a. 郑   人   袭   胡,   取之。(《史记》)

                 Zhèng   rén   xí   Hú   qǔ zhī

                 Zheng.State   people   attack   Hu.State   capture it

                 "The State of Zheng attacked and captured the State of Hu."

       b. 郑国   人   袭击   胡国,   把 它 夺取   了。

                                              (《史记》)

                 Zhèngguó   rén   xíjī   Húguó bǎ tā duóqǔ   le

                 Zheng.State   people   attack Hu.State BA it   capature ASP

                 "The State of Zheng attacked and captured the State of Hu."

In (92)a verbs expressing the meaning "attack" and "capture" are both represented by monosyllabic verbs 袭 xí "attack" and 取 qǔ "capture" in Old Chinese, but their Modern Chinese counterparts are both represented as disyllabic verbs 袭击 xíjī "attack" and 夺取 duóqǔ "capture" in (92)b.

The difference in the syllabic feature of verbs between Old and Modern

Chinese is also supported by the survey made by Shi (2002). In his study, Shi selects 124 verbs which appear in Pre-modern Chinese and survive in Modern Chinese. He traces the origin of these verbs in earlier texts and finds that 94% of his sample verbs entered Chinese lexicon in the period from the fifth century to twelfth century, namely after the Old Chinese period, which also indicates verbs in the Old Chinese period are mostly monosyllabic.

Different from Modern Chinese, Old Chinese is also reported to have more complicated phonological system and morphological derivation system. Wang (1980) observes that verbs with the same pronunciation in Modern Chinese may show contrastive features in initials, finals or tones in Old Chinese. More importantly, words in Old Chinese are attested to be derivable by changing the phonetic features of words. This process resembles some phonologically featured word derivation process in English, if the verb bleed is considered to be derived from the noun blood by changing the vowel or the verb record is derived from the noun record by changing the stress placement of the word (Packward, 1998). Some of the attested phonological derivation processes in Old Chinese are voicing, changing vowel quality and tone alternation (Downer, 1959; Wang, 1980; Norman, 1988; Baxter, 1992). Among them, tone alternation is the most clearly documented phonological derivation process, which is "the use of a change of tone to create a new word related in meaning to a base word" (Sun, 1997). In this process a new word is derived from a base word by changing its original tone which is one of the three tones 平声 píngshēng "level tone", 上声 shàngshēng "rising tone" and 入声 rùshēng "entering tone" to the forth tone 去声 qùshēng "departing tone". However, it is worth noting that the relationship between such tonally derived word pairs is not fixed. They may be contrastive with each other by differences in varied semantic or grammatical properties. Some commonly documented derivation processes through tone alternation involve nouns to verbs, intransitive to transitive or causative derivation. Example word pairs involving derivation through tone alternation are given in Table 3. Most of the examples are from Packard (1998), with some words discussed by Sun (1997) also included. The phonetic forms of the example words are modified from the sources for consistency. The reconstruction of the pronunciation of Old Chinese is based on Guo (1986), and is transcribed into International Phonetic Alphabet. As the tones of Old Chinese are not exactly the same as those of Modern Chinese, instead of using tone markings on Pinyin, researchers studying Old Chinese phonology usually adopt a different transcription system for tones in Old Chinese for accuracy. The present study following Sun (1997) represents the four tones by adding half circles on the four sides of the word: 平 (level tone), 上 (rising tone), 入 (entering tone), and 去 (departing tone).

Table 3 Word Pairs Involving Derivation via Tone Alternation

Base Word	Gloss	Departing Tone Derived Word	Gloss
冠 kuan	"cap"	冠 kuan	"to cap"
王 ɣĭaŋ	"king"	王 ɣĭaŋ	"be king"
饭 bĭwan	"eat"	饭 bĭwan	"food"
好 xəu	"pretty"	好 xəu	"to love"
高 kau	"high"	高 kau	"height"
受 zĭəu	"receive"	授 zĭəu	"give"
下 ɣea	"go down"	下 ɣea	"lower"
上 zĭaŋ	"ascend"	上 zĭaŋ	"above, top"

It can be seen in the table the tone derivation process involves various grammatical functions such as noun to verb (e.g 冠, 王), adjective to noun (e.g. 高), and intransitive to transitive verb (e. g. 下) derivations. The Chinese characters representing the base and derived forms are usually the same or differ only minimally, with the same component reflecting their cognate relation (Packard, 1998).

The contrast in grammatical functions between words with the original tone and its counterpart with derived departing tone can be attested in Old Chinese data. For example, the grammatical difference between the base verb and the derived verb 下 are illustrated in example sentences in (93).

(93) a. 日　之　西　矣，　牛　羊　下　　　来。(《诗经》)

rì　zhī　xī　yǐ　niú　yang　**xià (ᶜɣɛɑ)**　lái

sun go.to west PART cattle sheep **go.down** come

"The sun has gone west, and cattle and sheep have come down."

b. 其　君　能　下　　　人，　必　　　能 (《左传》)

qí　jūn　néng　**xià (ɣɛɑˀ)**　rén　bì　néng

his king can **lower** people definitely can

信　用　　　　其　民　矣。(《左传》)

xìn　yòng　qí　mín　yǐ

trust take.advantage.of his people PART

"The king humbled himself before his people, so he would definitely win the trust of his people."

As Sun (1997) explains, in (93)a the base verb 下 is read in departing tone represented as ᶜɣɛɑ, and in this case it is an intransitive verb meaning "go down", but when it is read in departing tone represented as ɣɛɑˀ in (93)b it becomes a transitive verb meaning "to cause to go down, lower".

As in most cases of phonological derivation process the derived new word and the base word are represented by the same written form, and along the diachronic evolution of Chinese language its phonological system has greatly simplified, the similarity and difference between pairs of words with derivational relation are often blurred. However, phonological derivation process provides important evidence for understanding the lexical semantics of verbs in Old Chinese.

Another typological property of Old Chinese is that similar to Modern Chinese, Old Chinese also allows serial verb constructions, which can be defined as "a sentence that contains two or more verb phrases or clauses juxtaposed without any marker indicating what the relationship is between them" (Li, Thompson, 1981). In serial verb constructions in Old Chinese, verbs may be used in isolating positions with each verb having its independent argument configuration or in contiguous positions usually with two parallel verbs sharing a common argument structure. One example of the former case is given in (94)a and the latter in (94)b.

(94) a. 击　李　由　军　破　　之。(《史记》)
　　　 jī　Lǐ　Yóu　jūn　pò　　zhī
　　　 attack Li You army destroy it
　　　 "He attacked Li You's army and destroyed it."

　　 b. 陈余　　击　　走　常山　　　王　　张耳。(《史记》)
　　　 Chén Yú jī　　zǒu Chángshān wáng Zhāng Ěr
　　　 Chen Yu attack run Changshan king Zhang Er
　　　 "Chen Yu attacked (and caused) Zhang Er the Changshan King
　　　 to run."

In (94)a the verbs 击 jī "attack" and 破 pò "destroy" are used in isolating positions, and each has its own objects. As long as the events described by these verbs happen in sequence logically, almost any verb can be used in this construction. In (94)b the verbs 击 jī "attack" and 走 zǒu "run" also co-occur in a single sentence without any morphological marker, but they are used in contiguous positions sharing a common argument structure, i.e. both verbs take the subject 陈余 Chén Yú "Chen Yu" and the object 常山王张耳 Chángshān Wáng Zhāng Ěr "Changshan King Zhang Er" as their own arguments. This kind of construction is also called a parallel construct (Sun, 2013). Note that though both types of constructions are considered serial verb constructions by Li and Thompson (1981), they demonstrate different grammatical properties. The first type like (94)a may be bi-clausal expressing separate events. That is why the construction poses fewer constraints on types of verbs that may appear in it. The second type like (94)b is generally considered mono-clausal, because it takes exactly two verbs which share all their arguments and cannot be separated by other elements. In particular, if the construction is modified by adverbs, both verbs are modified simultaneously. This can be seen in (95).

(95) 尽　　　除　　　去　　　先　　　帝　　　之　　　故　　　臣……

(《史记》)

jìn　　chú　　qù　　xiān　dì　　zhī　　gù　　chén

completely remove get.rid.of former emperor POSS original vassal

"(He) completely replaced the former emperor's original vassals..."

In (95), the adverb 尽 jìn "completely" appears before both verbs 除 chú "remove" and 去 qù "get rid of" which form the serial verb constructions. It can neither be inserted between the two verbs nor can be understood as modifying only the former or the latter verb. Thus it is evident that the two verbs are used in a single clause.

The serial verb construction in Old Chinese and a careful distinction between different subtypes of this construction can help examine the lexical semantics of verbs in Old Chinese. It will be further explained as to the methodology and data in examining Old Chinese verbs.

4.1.2 Motion Events in Old Chinese

As to the typology of motion events, Old Chinese is believed to be a verb-framed language (Peyraube, 2006; Ma, 2008; Shi, Wu, 2014, 2015). Its typological properties as a verb-framed language can be attested from both its language structure and language use. As to language structure, the path is prototypically rendered into main verbs of the sentence as can be seen in (96). The path of the motion events are encoded into one-syllable verbs 入 rù "enter" and 出 chū "exit" specifying the direction of motion.

(96) 姜　入　于室，与　崔子　自　侧　户　出。(《左传》)

Jiāng rù　yú shì　yǔ　Cuīzǐ　zì　cè　hù　chū

Jiang **enter** at　room with Cuizi from side door **exit**

"Jiang entered the room and exited the side door with Cuizi."

Concerning language use, Old Chinese is observed to have a larger path lexicon and path verbs are also used more frequently than manner verbs. Ma (2008) collects 75 Old Chinese motion verbs from six Old Chinese texts and finds that while pure manner verbs only count a small part of the entire motion lexicon (14%), pure path verbs count the majority of the whole (61%). As to the token of constructions used in Old Chinese, Shi and Wu (2014) in their study of six Old Chinese texts also point out an obvious asymmetry towards path verbal constructions. The percentage of pure manner verbal constructions is about 11.17% of all motion constructions, but the percentage of pure path verbal constructions is about 74.53%. Thus from the aspects of both language structure and language use, Old Chinese demonstrates typological features of the verb-framed languages. It is important to take the properties of this framing type of Old Chinese into account when the lexical semantics of verbs is examined.

4.2   Research Method and Data

One of the most often used methods to determine a verb's lexical semantics and grammatical behaviors in Modern Chinese, linguistic tests, cannot be extended to Old Chinese, since Old Chinese is practically a dead language and the lexical semantics and grammatical behaviors of a verb in Old Chinese cannot be judged directly through native speakers' intuition, and in particular, negative evidence cannot be provided directly by linguistic tests. Though this problem makes the study of Old Chinese verbs more difficult, it is not impossible to reveal the properties of the lexicalization patterns of Old Chinese verbs. One way to investigate a verb's lexical semantics and grammatical behaviors in Old Chinese is to check its compatibility with other elements with certain grammatical features observed in data examples in authentic corpora. As to the study of manner or result verbs in motion events, it is indeed a plausible way to analyze their ontological type and relevant grammatical behaviors. Levin and Rapapport Hovav (2015) note that "the conceptual component which is lexicalized in the verb can be identified by determining which facet of the event the verb restricts". They further illustrate the point with the grammatical behaviors of English verbs. The verb "move" can be used to describe the motion of any kind along any path in any kind of manner, because besides the meaning of motion itself the verb lexicalizes neither manner nor path information. Once a verb lexicalizes another conceptual component, the events that it can describe are accordingly restricted. If the verb lexicalizes the path, it imposes restrictions on the path of motion that can be described by the construction the verb is used in. Alternatively, if the verb lexicalizes a manner it necessarily restricts the manner, but not the path of the event it can be used to describe. Thus manner and path verbs show different compatibilities with other elements expressing manner and path in the same motion construction. For example, sentences in (97) with the English verbs enter and walk illustrate this point.

(97) a. John entered running/walking/jogging.

b. John walked into/out of/around the house.

As shown in (97)a, enter necessarily expresses a path that ends in some space, but it does not restrict the manner of the motion, so it is compatible with different manner adverbials "running", "walking", and "jogging". In contrast, walk necessarily refers to a specific way of moving, but it does not impose restrictions on the path of the motion, so it is compatible with a wide range of path information such as "into", "out of" and "around". The same is also true of Old Chinese verbs. Based on the authentic corpus of Old Chinese, checking the compatibility with other elements describing manner or path information, manner or path verbs can be identified in a reliable way.

However, there is a key difference between English and Old Chinese. In English, if one conceptual component of motion, manner or result, is expressed as the verb of the sentence, the other concept will be expressed outside the verb as adverbials, particles or prepositions, but Old Chinese, as discussed in Section 4.1.1, allows serial verb constructions, in which both components may be expressed as verbs at the same time. Thus it can be predicted that manner and path verbs in serial verb constructions must have different compatibility with other verbs expressing manner or path information. This makes it possible to determine a verb's ontological category. To be specific, I will determine the ontological category of Old Chinese verbs as manner or path by checking their distribution and conpatibility with other verbs in serial verb constructions. Based on the properties of manner and path verbs discussed so far, the criteria used to judge the comceptual components encoded in Old Chinese motion verbs are as follows: in Old Chinese data, only manner verbs are compatible with verbs expressing varied path information; only path verbs are compatible with verbs expressing varied manner information.

Note that the serial verb constructions used in the present studies are restricted to those describing a single integral motion event. If co-occurring verbs describe different motion events, in particular, as mentioned in Section 4.2.1, with respect to the situation where verbs are used in isolating positions, theoretically all verbs can co-occur in serial verb constructions, and then their compatibility has little to do with their lexical meaning. For example, in (98)a the two path verbs 出 chū "exit" and 归 guī "return" express two separate motion events which occur in sequence, i. e. the prince of Zhao firstly exited from the State of Qin and then he returned to his home the State of Zhao, so in spite of the fact that they lexicalize distinct directions of motion they can co-occur with each other in the serial verb construction without contradictions. Therefore, the target serial verb constructions I use are only restricted to those describing a single integral motion event as (98)b.

(98) a. 赵　　太子　　出　归　　国。(《史记》)

　　　　Zhào tàizǐ　　chū guī　　guó

　　　　Zhao prince **exit return** state

　　　　"The prince of Zhao exited (from the State of Qin) and returned to his home the Sate of Zhao."

　　b. 张　　耳 与　赵　王　歇 走入　　巨鹿 城。(《史记》)

　　　　Zhāng Ěr yǔ　Zhào wáng Xiē **zǒu rù**　　Jùlù chéng

　　　　Zhang Er with Zhao Xie.king　**run enter** Julu town

　　　　"Zhang Er and Zhao Xie the King ran into Julu town."

In (98)b with the verb 入 rù "enter" expressing the path and the verb 走 zǒu "run" specifying the particular manner in which the whole event is executed, what they describe is just two accompanying parts of an integral event. In fact, only in this kind of serial constructions can the co-occurrence of components be accounted by the compatibility of their lexical semantics, since a single event cannot be carried out with two distinct manners or in two distinct directions.

In addition, whether a serial verb construction describes a single motion event can also be determined by the temporal contouring the subevents involve. That is, if the subevents described by the verbs in a serial construction occur within the same time contour, they are regarded as a single motion event, otherwise they are not. For instance, in (98)a, the two subevents described by the two verbs 出 chū "exit" and 归 guī "return" do not occur within the same time span; rather they occur in sequence, so they are not regarded as a single event. In contrast, in (98)b the subevents described by the two verbs 走 zǒu "run" and 入 rù "enter" occur within the same time span; they unfold together, so they necessarily describe a single event.

The analysis presented in this part is based on attested data drawn from representative Chinese texts from the Old Chinese period (BC 500–AD 200). The reasons why only texts from the Old Chinese period are chosen are as follows. First, since the Chinese language has undergone radical changes since the Old Chinese period, with most distinct typological features of verb-framed language (Ma, 2008; Shi, Wu, 2015), lexical semantics and grammatical properties of motion verbs selected from texts composed in Old Chinese times must differentiate those in Modern Chinese to the largest degree, which will help check whether the MRC applies to a typologically different language. Second, to make the data more comparable to those in Modern Chinese, it is better to look at the lexicalization patterns of verbs within certain synchronic period, as data ranging a long period of history may not show consistent lexicalization features themselves. I have mainly examined the actual uses of motion verbs in two Old Chinese books《左传》and《史记》, but when necessary, I also make reference to other books composed in the same period of time. These books include《论语》,《荀子》,《管子》,《韩非子》,《吕氏春秋》and《战国策》. All example sentences mentioned in this part are from books composed in the Old Chinese period. I mainly get access to these data via a diachronic corpus of Chinese books named 汉籍全文检索系统 developed by Shaanxi Normal University. With respect to the quoted example sentences, I have also looked up the hard copy books to ensure the accuracy of those examples.

4.3 Lexicalization Patterns of Motion Verbs in Old Chinese

4.3.1 Preliminary Classification of Motion Verbs in Old Chinese

Focusing on 75 verbs collected by Ma (2008) from six representative texts composed in the Old Chinese period and with reference to her analysis of these verbs, I will first make a preliminary classification of these motion verbs. Ma classifies these verbs into three groups: manner verbs, path verbs and manner plus path verbs. Example verbs of each type are listed in (99).

(99) a. Directed motion/path verbs

之 zhī "go",   入 rù "enter"   归 guī"return"

反 fǎn "return"   至 zhì "arrive"   往 wǎng "go.to"

退 tuì "retreat"   上 shàng "ascend"

下 xià "descend"   出 chū "exit"

b. Manner-of-motion verbs

驰 chí "gallop"   迁 qiān "move"   徙 xǐ "move"

游 yóu "tour"   翔 xiáng "fly"   旅 lǚ "travel"

驱 qū "drive (a horse, a cart, etc.)"

c. Manner plus path verbs

走 zǒu "run"   奔 bēn "rush"   逃 táo "flee"

亡 wáng "flee"   济 jì "sail across" 涉 shè "sail across"

(Ma, 2008)

In my analysis, I will first examine the verbs in (99)a and (99)b to see whether they conform to the MRC in terms of their lexical semantics and grammatical behaviors. Since Ma (2008) claims that verbs in (99)c encode both manner and path meaning components, if she is correct, they will pose a real challenge for the MRC hypothesis, so following the analysis of the first two group of verbs, the verbs in (99)c will be analyzed in detail to see whether they indeed lexicalize the two components manner and path simultaneously violating the MRC hypothesis.

The result of the analysis of the first two groups of verbs in (99)a and (99)b is consistent with my hypothesis: their syntactic distributions show typical properties of manner and result verbs respectively. Verbs in (99)a are all manner verbs, so in Old Chinese data they are attested to co-occur with verbs expressing varied path information. Verbs in (99)b are all path verbs, so they are found to appear with verbs describing different manners of the motion. For example, the actual uses of the path verb 出 chū "exit" and the manner verb 趋 qū "hurry up" given in (100) and (101) illustrate this clearly.

(100) a. **走 出**，遇 贼 于 门。(《左传》)
      zǒu chū yù zéi yú mén
      run exit meet rebel at gate
      "(He) ran out and met rebels at the gate."

    b. 孔子 **趋 出**，以 语 子贡……(《荀子》)
      Kǒngzǐ **qū chū** yǐ yù Zǐgòng
      Confucius **hurry.up exit** with tell Zigong
      "Confucius hurried out, and told (it) to Zigong..."

    c. 楚昭 王 **亡 出** 郢，奔 郧。(《史记》)
      Chǔzhāo wáng **wáng chū** Yǐng bēn Yún
      Chuzhao king **flee exit** Ying rush Yun
      "The King Zhao of Chu fled from Ying and went to Yun."

As can be seen from (100), the directed motion verb 出 chū "exit" only lexicalizes the path information without specifying the manner of motion in its lexical semantics, so it is compatible with a variety of verbs such as 走 zǒu "run",

趋 qū "hurry up" and 亡 wáng "flee", which express different manners of motion.

In contrast, the manner verb 趋 qū "hurry up" show different co-occurring properties with other verbs. It only lexicalizes the way how the motion is carried out, but does not specify the direction of motion, so it is compatible with varied path verbs in serial verb constructions. As illustrated in (101), it may co-occur with varied path verbs such as 进 jìn "move forward", 过 guò "pass", and 退 tuì "retreat".

(101) a. 卫侯　　　怒，　　　王孙贾　　　趋　　　进。(《左传》)

　　　 Wèi hóu   nù   Wáng Sūnjiǎ qū   jìn

　　　 Wèi Duke get.furious Wang Sunjia **hurry.up move.forward**

　　　 "The Duke of Wei got furious; Wang Sunjia hurried forward."

　　b. 姜　　怒，　　　公子　偃、公子　鉏　趋　　　过。

　　　　　　　　　　　　　　　　　　　　　　　　　(《左传》)

　　　 Jiāng nù   Gōngzǐ Yǎn Gōngzǐ Chú qū   guò

　　　 Jiang get.furious Gongzi Yan Gongzi Chu **hurry.up pass**

　　　 "Jiang got furious; Gongzi Yan and Gongzi Chu hurried past."

　　c. 申丰　　　趋　　退，　归，　尽室　将　行。

　　　　　　　　　　　　　　　　　　　　　　　(《左传》)

　　　 Shēnfēng qū   tuì   guī jìn shì   jiāng xíng

　　　 Shenfeng **hurry.up recede** return all family will   move

　　　 "Shenfeng hurried backward. He returned home planning to go away with the whole family."

Therefore, it is clear that based on their compatibility with different types of information, manner and path verbs in (99)a and (99)b show consistent grammatical behaviors with their counterparts in Modern Chinese, exhibiting distinct grammatical hallmarks of manner or result verbs. In serial verb constructions manner-of-motion verbs are compatible with varied path verb, while directed motion verbs can co-occur with different manner verbs. In next section, I will have a close look at the verbs in (99)c to check whether they are counterexample verbs to the MRC.

4.3.2 Purported Counterexamples to the MRC in Old Chinese

If the problems of some potential counterexamples to the MRC in Modern Chinese could be solved easier, the lexical principle MRC faces even bigger challenges in Old Chinese, as researchers (Ma, 2008; Shi, Wu, 2014) claim that verbs encoding both manner and direction of motion in Old Chinese have systematic distributions. When discussing the way Old Chinese encodes path in motion events, Ma (2008) argues that besides the wide use of "pure path verbs" there are a group of manner-of-motion verbs which also have path implicitly encoded at the same time. Similarly, adopting a notion from Yang (2005), Shi and Wu (2014) call this kind of verbs "semantically synthetic verbs", since according to them these manner verbs encode path information as well. Some problematic verbs cited by these researchers are listed in (102).

> (102) 走 zǒu "run"　　　奔 bēn "rush"　　　趋 qū "hurry up"
>
> 　　　涉 shè "sail across"　济 jì "sail across"　逃 táo "flee"
>
> 　　　亡 wáng "flee"　　　遁 dùn "flee"

The evidence used by Ma (2008) and Shi and Wu (2014) to support their argument is the same, i. e. without other path-indicating elements in the sentence these manner verbs can take noun phrases directly as their arguments to describe the direction of motion, as illustrated in (103).

> (103) a. 怀　王　恐，　乃　从　间道　走　赵 (《史记》)
>
> 　　　huái wáng kǒng nǎi cóng jiāndào zǒu Zhào
>
> 　　　Huai king scare hence via byway **walk Zhao.State**
>
> 　　　以　　求　　归。
>
> 　　　yǐ　　qiú　　guī
>
> 　　　in.order.to seek　return

"The King Huai was so scared that he went to the State of Zhao via a byway to seek returning to his home state under the escort of the State of Zhao."

b. 王子　　克 **奔**　燕。(《左传》)

Wángzǐ Kè **bēn** Yān

Prince Ke **rush** Yan.State

"Prince Ke rushed to the State of Yan."

c. 故　　昔　　樊於期　　**逃** **秦**　之 燕。(《史记》)

gù　　xī　　Fán.Yú qī **táo** **Qín**　zhī Yān

hence in.the.past Fan Yuqi **flee Qin.State** go Yan.State

"Hence in the past Fan Yuqi fled from the State of Qin and went to the State of Yan."

In (103), without other path-indicating elements in the sentence, the manner verbs 走 zǒu "run", 奔 bēn "rush" and 逃 táo "flee" are all followed directly by noun phrases which indicate the direction of motion.

In addition, as observed by scholars (e.g. Ma, 2008), these verbs show a clear contrast with other manner verbs (e.g. 行 xíng "move", 驰 chí "gallop", 骋 chěng "gallop"), which always need overt path-indicating elements to be expressed when they are used in motion events describing the direction of motion with reference to ground. For example, as shown in (104) when the manner verb 驰 chí "gallop" is used in a motion construction where path information is also encoded, path verbs such as 往 wǎng "go to", 归 guī "return", 入 rù "enter", etc., are needed to relate the manner verb 驰 chí "gallop" to its ground information.

(104) a. (汉王)　　还　至　定陶，**驰**　**入**　齐王　壁。

(《史记》)

Hàn wáng huán zhì Dìngtáo **chí**　**rù**　Qí wáng bì

Han king　return arrive Dingtao **gallop enter** Qi king barracks

"(The King of Han) returned to Dingtao and galloped to the barracks of the King of Qi."

b. 相如　　乃　　与　　驰　　归　　成都。(《史记》)

Xiàngrú nǎi　yǔ　chí　guī　Chéngdū

Xiangru hence with **gallop return** Chengdu

"Xiangru then galloped back to Chengdu with (her)."

c. 太子　闻　之，驰　　往，　伏　　尸 (《史记》)

tàizǐ　wén zhī chí　**wǎng** fú　shī

prince hear it　**gallop go.to** prostrate dead.body

而　哭，极　　哀。

ér　kū　jí　āi

CONJ cry　extremely sad

"The prince heard it. He galloped there and prostrated himself over the dead body crying very sadly."

However, there is an obvious problem with their analysis, i.e. the existence or non-existence of overt path-indicating elements in the sentence is not a reliable way to decide whether a verb encodes path or not. On the one hand, under certain circumstances overt path-indicating elements may be omitted due to varied reasons (Lin, 2011). On the other hand, even with overt path-indicating elements the verb's ontological category cannot be determined simply, since not only manner verbs but also path verbs can be followed by path-indicating elements. For example, both of the verbs 入 rù "enter" and 游 yóu "tour" can be followed by the preposition 于 yú before they take noun phrases, but the two verbs belong to different categories, as illustrated in (105).

(105) a. 蔡侯　　入　于　敝邑　以　　　行。(《左传》)

Cài hóu　rù　yú bì yì　yǐ　　xíng

Cai Duke **enter at**　my town in.order.to move

"The Duke of Cai entered my town in order to go (to the State of Jin)."

b. 卫侯　　**游** 于　郊，　　子南　仆。(《左传》)

Wèi hóu **yóu yú**　jiāo　　Zǐnán　pú

Wei Duke **tour yu**　suburb　Zinan　drive.a.cart

"The Duke of Wei had Zinan drive a cart traveling around in the suburb."

In (105)a, the verb 入 rù "enter" is a pure path verb describing a directed motion as moving from outside to inside of a reference object, while in (105)b, 游 yóu "tour" is a prototypical manner verb meaning "travel or tour around". Therefore, the existence or non-existence of the preposition 于 yú in the sentence is not a reliable way to determine the ontological category of the verbs 入 rù "enter" and 游 yóu "tour".

Thus in order to decide whether these verbs are indeed counterexamples to the MRC, a more careful investigation is needed. In the remainder of this section, I will look up the actual uses of these verbs in the corpus of Old Chinese trying to clarify their categorization and find out whether they are counterexamples to the MRC. Based on their actual uses, I suggest that these verbs actually lexicalize either manner or path in each use and thus conform to the MRC. Though these verbs seem to encode path and manner of motion, their manner and path information are derived from different sources, i. e. not both manner and path information are lexicalized in the verb itself simultaneously. To be specific, these verbs can be divided into 3 groups: (1) polysemous motion verbs with manner and path senses always encoded complementarily (e.g. 走 zǒu "run", 奔 bēn "rush", 趋 qū "hurry up"), (2) manner verbs with the path meaning component derived from the contexts (e.g 逃 táo "escape", 亡 wáng "escape", 遁 dùn "escape"), and (3) path verbs with the manner meaning component derived from the contexts (e. g. 涉 shè "sail across", 济 jì "sail across"). Generally, the grammatical behaviors of these verbs in Old Chinese corpus support this analysis. I will look at them group by group.

4.3.2.1 Motion Verbs with Separate Manner or Result Sense 走 zǒu "run", 奔 bēn "rush", and 趋 qū "hurry up"

The primary lexical meaning of the verbs 走 zǒu "run", 奔 bēn "rush", and 趋 qū "hurry up" in Old Chinese reflects the conceptualization of the manner of motion such as the gait or the speed of the movement. An example sentence in which 走 zǒu "run" specifies the manner of motion is provided in (106) below.

(106) 荀　跞　掩　　耳　而　　　走。(《左传》)

　　　Xún Lì　yǎn　ěr　ér　　zǒu

　　　Xun Li cover ears CONJ run

　　　"Xun Li ran with his hands covering his ears."

As in this case it only encodes the manner of motion, it is compatible with varied path information. As illustrated in (107), the verb 走 zǒu "run" is compatible with path information such as 反 fǎn "return", 周 zhōu "around" and 循 xún "move along" to express varied directions of motion.

(107) a. 弃疾　使　　周　　　走　而　　呼。(《左传》)

　　　　Qìjí　shǐ　zhōu　zǒu ér　　hū

　　　　Qiji cause **around run** CONJ shout

　　　　"Qiji made people run around and shout."

　　　b. **循**　　　墙　而　　**走**, 亦　莫　余　敢　侮。

　　　　　　　　　　　　　　　　　　　　　　　　(《左传》)

　　　　xún　　　qiáng ér　　zǒu yì　mò　yú　gǎn　wǔ

　　　　move.along wall　CONJ **run**　also NEG me dare bully

　　　　"(I) ran along the wall and nobody dared to bully me."

　　　c. 纣　　　反　　走 登　　鹿台 (《史记》)

　　　　zhòu　　fǎn　zǒu dēng Lùtái

　　　　Zhou.king **return run** mount Lutai

"King Zhou ran back and mounted Lutai"

Nevertheless, as mentioned above in Old Chinese these verbs may take locative nouns directly as their argument. Researchers (Ma, 2008; Shi, Wu, 2014) take it as evidence that these verbs lexicalize both manner and path information of the motion. As can be seen in (108), the verb 走 zǒu "run" can be immediately followed by locative nouns which act as the goal argument of the verb. Since there is no other element in the sentence to express the path information, the verb seems to encode both manner and direction of motion and thus constitute a counterexample to the MRC.

(108) a. 齐侯   驾，   将 走 游棠。(《左传》)
　　　Qí hóu jià   jiāng zǒu Yóutáng
　　　Qi Duke ride.chariot will **run Youtang**
　　　"The Duke of Qi rode a chariot and wanted to run to Youtang."

　　　b. 百濮 离   居， 将 各 走 其 邑。(《左传》)
　　　Bǎipú lí   jū jiāng gè zǒu qí yì
　　　Baipu scattered live will each **run his town**
　　　"People of Baipu live in scattered communities and they would go back to their own town."

Nonetheless, a careful analysis of 走 zǒu "run" shows that when it takes a locative noun as its argument it does lexicalize the path of motion, but at the same time it also undergoes an ontological shift from a manner verb to a path one only lexicalizing the directed motion as "go to". There are mainly two pieces of evidence which support my argument.

First, when 走 zǒu "run" is followed by a locative noun, it undergoes tone alternation to be read in the fourth tone 去声 qùshēng "departing tone", which can be regarded as a morphological marking of its categorical change. As discussed in Section 4.1.1, tone alternation is a productive way of word formation in Old

Chinese. In his study of the tone alternation of words in Old Chinese, Sun (1997) argues that words represented by the same Chinese character but differentiated by distinct tones should be treated as separate lexical entries with different lexical meanings. He analyzes 走 zǒu "run" in detail and demonstrates that for lexicalizing the goal of the motion, the verb is always read in departing tone. The sentence pair in (109) illustrates the tone difference when 走 zǒu "run" is used as a pure manner verb in (109)a or a path verb in (109)b.

(109) a. 荀　跞　掩　耳　而　　走。(《左传》)

Xún Lì yǎn ěr ér zǒu (ᶜtso)

Xun Li cover ears CONJ run

"Xun Li ran with his hand covering his ears."

b. 赵　旃　弃　车　而　　走　　　林……(《左传》)

Zhào Zhān qì chē ér zǒu (tsoˀ) lín

Zhao Zhan abandon cart CONJ run forest

"Zhao Zhan abandoned his cart and ran to the forest..."

In (109)a, 走 zǒu "run" is used as a pure manner verb, and it is read in rising tone, which is reconstructed in International Phonetic Alphabet as ᶜtso, but in (109)b when it is used as a path verb followed by a locative noun, it is read in departing tone, which is represented as tsoˀ. Because the alternation in the tone is consistent with its change in lexical semantics and syntactic distribution, the tone change can be regarded as a morphological marker of its ontological shift.

Wang (2013) also analyzes the semantic relation between pairs of motion verbs, which have derivational relation through tone change in Old Chinese. She argues that when read in departing tone, the originally boundless manner verbs like 走 zǒu "run", 奔 bēn "rush" and 趋 qū "hurry up" become bounded motion verbs. In other words, the boundless manner-of-motion verbs derivate motion verbs with the goal direction of "go to" (Sun, 1997; Wang, 2013) by changing the phonetic feature of tone, which changes the motion from a non-scalar change to a bounded two-point scalar change. As discussed in Chapter 2, as to hallmarks of manner and result verbs in general, though not all path verbs are bounded motion verbs (e. g. descend and ascend are boundless path verbs), bounded motion verbs are certainly path verbs, as manner verbs are aspectually unbounded and durative. While Sun (1997) and Wang (2013) do not state explicitly these verbs have undergone an ontological category change from manner to path verbs via tone change, the difference in lexical meaning between the base verb and the derived verb which they note certainly confirms this fact.

Moreover, the fact that the verb 走 zǒu "run" undergoes a shift as to its ontological category can also be attested by its semantic entailment when it takes a locative noun directly. While the use of 走 zǒu "run" as a manner verb always requires the theme to be animate, since it is a prototypical self-agentive motion verb describing the motion of human beings in particular, it is not necessarily the case for its use as a path verb. Zhang (2005) observes that when indicating the direction of motion, the action expressed by 走 zǒu "run" is not restricted to any specific way of moving and it only describes a goal-directed motion. In Old Chinese texts, the most often used goal argument of 走 zǒu "run" is the names of places or states such as 莒 Jǔ "County Ju", 鲁 Lǔ "the State of Lu", 秦 Qín "the State of Qin", etc.; the themes of the motion are very often people across all walks of life. Judging from the contexts, the involved manner of motion is not restricted to "running using legs" or any specific type of motion. For instance, according to the contexts, the ways of motion involved in (110) are all different.

(110) a. 齐 侯 驾,　　　将 走 游棠。(《左传》)

Qí hóu jià　　　jiāng zǒu Yóutang

Qi Duke ride.chariot will　run Youtang

"The Duke of Qi rode a chariot and wanted to run to Youtang."

b. 长史 欣 恐, 还 走 其 军。(《史记》)

Zhǎng shǐ Xīn kǒng huán zǒu qí jūn

Zhangshi Xin scare return run his army

"Zhangshi Xin scared and returned to his army."

c. 始皇　　　三十七　　年　冬……北　走　琅邪。

(《史记》)

Shǐ huáng　sānshíqī　nián dōng běi　zǒu Lángyá

Emperor Shi thirty seventh year winter north run Langya

"In the thirty seventh year Emperor Shi … went in the north
direction to Langya."

In (110)a 齐侯 Qí hóu "the Duke of Qi" rode a chariot; in (110)b 长史欣
Zhǎngshǐ Xīn "Zhangshi Xin" probably rode a horse; and in (110)c 始皇 Shǐ Huáng
"Emperor Shi" probably traveled in a sedan chair. Thus it is clear that when used as
a directed motion verb, 走 zǒu "run" does not encode the manner of motion.

Sun (1997) also notes that when used in directed motion sense the subject of
走 zǒu "run" can be inanimate, which provides further evidence for the dropping
of the manner sense in the lexical meaning of 走 zǒu "run". For example, as
illustrated in (111)a the subject of 走 zǒu "run" is an inanimate entity 新丰道
Xīnfēng Dào "Xinfeng Road", so in this case no manner sense can be possibly
encoded at all.

(111) a. 上　　　指示　　慎夫人　　　新丰　　道，曰：

shàng　zhǐshì　Shèn fūrén　Xīnfēng　Dào　yuē

Emperor indicate Shen Madam Xinfeng Road say

此 走 邯郸　　道　　也。(《史记》)

cǐ zǒu Hándān　Dào　yě

it run Handan　Road PART

"The emperor indicated Xinfeng Road to Madam Shen and
said this road went to Handan."

b. ……如水　之　　走　　下(《管子》)

rú　**shuǐ**　zhī　**zǒu**　xià

like   **water** POSS **run**   down

"...like water's tendency of going down"

Similarly, in (111)b, the subject of the motion is 水 shuǐ "water", so in this case no possible manner is encoded either. The unrestricted subject of the directed motion use of 走 zǒu "run" further confirms the fact that no manner is lexicalized in the verb.

To summarize, the actual uses of the verbs 走 zǒu "run", 奔 bēn "rush" and 趋 qū "hurry up" in Old Chinese texts indicate that they are primarily manner-of-motion verbs, which are compatible with varied path information and only express the specific way in which the motion is carried out. However, when they are followed directly by noun phrases to indicate the goal of motion, their altered phonetic property and lexical entailment demonstrate that they undergo an ontological shift from manner to path verbs. Therefore, they are not real challenges for the MRC hypothesis.

4.3.2.2 Manner Verbs with the Inferred Direction Sense 逃 táo "flee", 亡 wáng "flee", and 遁 dùn "flee"

Another group of verbs which are said to encode both manner and path information simultaneously are 逃 táo "flee", 亡 wáng "flee", and 遁 dùn "flee". I argue, however, these three verbs are all manner verbs and their directed motion sense arises from the pragmatic support from the contexts. Though all of the three verbs can be translated as the English verb "flee", they have distinct lexical meanings and grammatical behaviors from their counterparts in English. In Old Chinese, without prepositions or other path-indicating elements the three verbs can also take a locative noun as a reference object for the motion they specify. As shown in (112), the verb 逃 táo "flee" takes the locative noun 秦 Qín "the State of Qin" directly without an explicit path-indicating element in between.

(112) 故   昔   樊於期   逃   秦   之 燕。(《史记》)
　　 gù   xī   Fán Yúqī táo Qín   zhī Yān
　　 hence in.the.past Fan Yuqi **flee** **Qin.State** go Yan.State

"Hence in the past Fan Yuqi fled from the State of Qin and went to the State of Yan."

The same is true of the other two verbs 亡 wáng "flee" and 遁 dùn "flee", as they can also be followed by locative nouns immediately, as shown in (113).

(113) a. 项羽　　击　　汉，拔　　荥阳，　　汉　兵

Xiàng Yǔ jī　　Hàn bá　　Xíngyáng　　Hàn bīng

Xiàng Yu attack Han capture Xingyang.town Han soldier

遁　　保巩……(《史记》)

dùn　Bǎogǒng

flee　Baogong.town

"Xiang Yu captured Xingyang, and soldiers of Han fled to Baogong..."

b. 伍子胥　之　**亡　楚**　　而　如　吴　也……

(《史记》)

Wǔ Zǐxū zhī **wáng Chǔ**　ér　rú　Wú　yě

Wu Zixu POSS **flee　Chu.State** CONJ go.to Wu.State PART

"Wu Zixu fled from the State of Chu and went to the State of Wu..."

As to these cases, Lin (2011) also argues that these verbs only lexicalize the manner of motion. She proposes that the locative nouns following these manner verbs may not be the arguments of these verbs; rather they may be the arguments of the omitted preposition 于/於 yú. She explains that in Old Chinese the preposition 于/於 yú may be omitted for varied reasons. She also presents different example sentences using the verb 逃 táo "flee" in the texts composed in the same period with and without the preposition 于/於 yú, as illustrated in (114)a and (114)b.

(114) a. 伍子胥 逃 楚　　而　之 吴。(《战国策》)

　　　　Wǔ Zǐxū **táo Chǔ**　ér　zhī　Wú

　　　　Wu Zixu **flee Chu.State** CONJ go.to Wu.State

　　　　"Wu zixu fled from the State of Chu and then arrived in the
　　　　State of Wu."

　　b. 桓 公　　之　难,　　管 仲　　　逃 于 鲁。

　　　　　　　　　　　　　　　　　　　　　　(《战国策》)

　　　　Huán Gōng zhī　nán　　Guǎn Zhòng **táo　yú** Lǔ

　　　　Huan Lord POSS difficulty Guan Zhong **flee　to** Lu.State

　　　　"When Lord Huan was in difficulty, Guan Zhong fled to the
　　　　State of Lu."

However, there is a problem with Lin's analysis. If the locative noun is indeed the argument of an omitted preposition 于/於 yú, the direction of motion encoded by two kinds of verbal constructions, i.e. the cases in which 逃 táo "flee" is followed by 于/於 yú or not, should be the same. However, it is not the case. In (114)a, when there is no preposition in between, the locative noun is the source of the motion, but in (114)b when there is the preposition 于/於 yú inserted, the locative noun is the goal of the motion. Thus Lin's argument that the locative noun is the argument of the omitted 于/於 yú does not hold.

However, I agree with Lin that 逃 táo "flee", 亡 wáng "flee" and 遁 dùn "flee" only lexicalize the manner of motion, but I base this point on a different piece of evidence that these verbs are not associated with a consistent direction of motion, contrary to the hallmarks of path verbs. As manner verbs, when they take locative nouns directly, the direction of motion can only be inferred from the contexts. Depending on different contexts, 逃 táo "flee" is compatible with different directions of motion, source or goal. As can be seen from (114)a above, the direction that the verb 逃 táo "flee" is associated with is the source of motion, but in some other cases like (115), the locative noun is the goal of the motion.

(115) 使　　人　　索　　扁　　鹊,　已　　　逃秦　　　　矣。

(《韩非子》)

shǐ　　rén　　suǒ　　Biǎn Què yǐ　　　**táo Qín**　　　yǐ

make people seek Bian Que already **flee Qin.State** PART

"(Duke Huan) made people seek Bian Que, but he had fled to the State of Qin."

In addition, in serial verb constructions 逃 táo "flee" is also compatible with verbs encoding varied path information such as 归 guī "return", 来 lái "come", etc., as seen in (116). This is also the evidence for the fact that 逃 táo "flee" itself does not lexicalize the direction of motion at all.

(116) a. ……逃　　归　　其　国……(《左传》)

táo　　guī　　qí　guó

flee　return his country

"...(he) fled back to his country..."

b. 秋,　　郑詹　　　自　齐　　　逃来。

(《春秋公羊传》)

qiū　　Zhèng Zhān zì　Qí　　　**táo lái**

autumn Zheng Zhan from Qi.State **flee come**

"In the autumn Zheng Zhan came fleeing from the State of Qi."

In a summary, the problematic verbs such as 逃 táo "flee", 亡 wáng "flee", and 遁 dùn "flee" are in fact manner verbs, because they do not impose restrictions on path information they may co-occur with. When they are directly followed by locative nouns, the direction they encode can only be inferred from the contexts. Therefore, this group of verbs do not violate the lexical principle either.

4.3.2.3 Directed Motion Verbs with the Inferred Manner Sense 涉 shè "sail across" and 济 jì "sail across"

Shi and Wu (2014, 2015) cite 涉 shè "sail across" and 济 jì "sail across" as semantically synthetic verbs which are manner verbs but encode path information as well. Though they specify the path information encoded in the verb 涉 shè "sail across" and 济 jì "sail across" as "across", they do not explain what manner is encoded in these verbs exactly. I suggest that these verbs are actually directed motion verbs, and their manner sense is also inferred from the contexts.

For these two verbs 涉 shè "sail across" and 济 jì "sail across", one may argue that besides the path information "across", it also entails a motion in the medium of water which can be regarded as the manner of motion. However, I argue that the water medium cannot be regarded as manner information, and it is in fact the more elaborated path information of the motion. Concerning the properties of path lexicon of typologically different languages, Verkerk (2014) argues that despite a limited set of abstract directions such as endpoint (enter), source (exit), mid-point (pass, cross), typologically different languages may differ as to how abstractly or concretely they elaborate path of motion. While satellite-framed languages tend to have a limited set of abstract directions, verb-framed languages with a relatively larger path lexicon tend to "have path verbs that refer to a far more varied set of more or less abstract reference points for motion placed within an environment" (Verkerk, 2014). For instance, as she explains, Jahai, a Mon-Khmer language spoken in the Malay Peninsula, features verbs such as rkruk "to move along the main river (in both upstream and downstream directions)", piris "to move across the flow of water", dey "to move upstream on a tributary" and hec "to move downstream on a tributary" (Vererk, 2014). Though these verbs encode more elaborated path information, they are still path verbs. As a verb-framed language, Old Chinese also has a relatively larger path lexicon including some directed motion verbs with more elaborated path information such as 涉 shè "sail across" and 济 jì "sail across". The medium of motion should not be regarded as a separate manner sense.

Nonetheless, path verbs with more salient and elaborated path information are not exclusive to verb-framed languages. For example, compared with other abstract path verbs such as descend and ascend in English, path verbs fall and sink not only lexicalize downward path with reference to the gravity, but also encode the medium the motion occurs within, air or water. In spite of this more elaborated path

汉语位移动词中的方式结果互补性研究——共时与历时视角

| | | | | | | | | | | | The Manner/Result Complementarity in Chinese Motion Verbs: Synchronic and Diachronic Perspectives

information, the ontological category of fall and sink is still that of path verbs, as their grammatical behaviors completely conform to hallmarks of result verbs, as illustrated in (117).

(117) a.*The vase fell worthless.

　　 b. *The sailors sank the boat useless.

　　 c. The boat sank to the bottom of the river in 10 minutes.

　　 d. The boat sank for 10 minutes.

　　 e. The leaves fell for/in a month.

As can be seen in (117)a and (117)b, on the one hand, since they encode scalar changes, they cannot appear with a phrase denoting another scale. Though semantically it is plausible that as a result of its falling a vase becomes worthless, the verb fall cannot be followed by the second predicate "worthless". The same is true of sink, it does not allow another scale denoting predicate "useless" either. On the other hand, the changes they lexicalize involve multi-point scales, so they may be interpreted as atelic or telic based on the specific contexts exhibiting aspectual features typical to multi-point scalar changes as illustrated in (117)c–(117)e.

The two Old Chinese verbs 涉 shè "sail across" and 济 jì "sail across" can be analyzed in the same way. Though the medium of motion seem to be the manner of motion, it is in fact more elaborated path information, which can also be understood as an adverbial modifier (Rappaport Hovav, 2015) of the motion, since they do not denote an independent change and do not affect the grammatical behaviors of the verbs. Therefore, they are not counterexamples to the MRC either.

Noteworthily, based on Rappaport Hovav and Levin's (2010) original analysis, though verbs such as cross and traverse are often considered as path verbs, they do not specify the direction of the path and thus do not involve scalar changes. For example, the verb cross, as they explain, can be used to refer to the traversal of the English Channel both from England to France and from France to England. However, different from Rappaport Hovav and Levin's view, I take verbs like cross and traverse in English as well as 涉 shè "sail across" and 济 jì "sail across" in Old

Chinese all as directed motion verbs encoding scalar changes. According to Fleischhauer and Gamerschlag (2014), result verbs can be scalar even if not all of the scale parameters are lexically specified. They also point out that underspecified scales in verbs can be compensated by introducing a missing parameter by the context or by a scale-denoting argument. Verbs mentioned above just fall into a subtype of scalar-change verbs which underspecify the order of the scale, and instead this order can only be retrieved from the contexts.

Summarizing, this part analyzes the three groups of counterexamples to the MRC in Old Chinese in detail and provides evidence that in actual uses these verbs actually encode either manner or path, consistent to the lexical principle.

4.4 Summary

In spite of a big typological difference between Old and Modern Chinese, the lexicalization patterns of motion verbs from both periods conform to the MRC. This confirms the validity and status of the MRC as a cross-linguistic lexical principle that constrains how much meaning a root can potentially lexicalize. It also supports an approach to reveal grammatical behaviors of verbs via an analysis of verbs' the lexical semantics represented in the form of event structure decomposition. However, languages may differ in strategies and morphosyntacitc resources available to make up the lexicalization gap constrained by the lexical principle. Across languages, pragmatic inference from the contexts is a common strategy to fill the lexicalization gap. In addition, morphosyntactic resources available in typologically different languages may provide languages with language-specific devices to distinguish lexicon with different ontological categories. As discussed in this chapter, with a more complicated phonological and morphological system, changing the phonetic properties in Old Chinese is one of the effective morphosyntactic devices facilitating verbs to derive a new separate sense and to distinguish the manner and path sense from each other.

Chapter 5

The Diachronic Evolution of Polysemous Motion Verbs

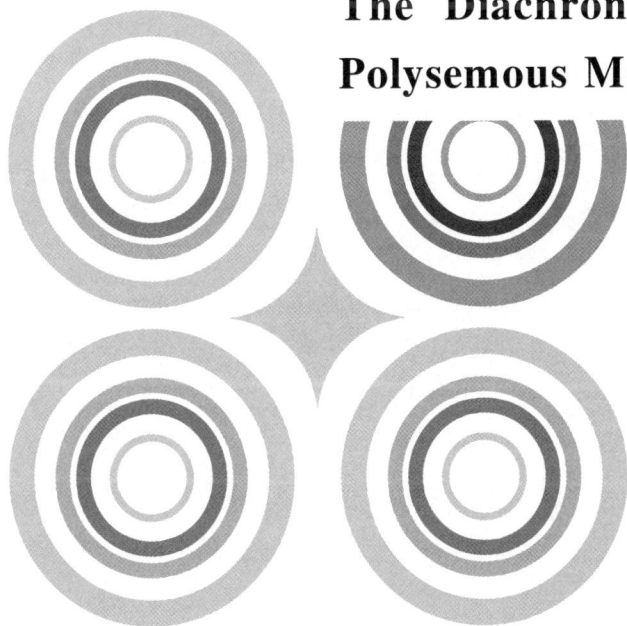

In Chapter 3 and Chapter 4, meaning components encoded in motion verbs in Modern and Old Chinese have been analyzed in detail and it is found that as to the lexicalized meaning components in verbs, manner and result meaning components cannot be encoded simultaneously. Thus the lexicalization patterns of motion verbs in Old and Modern Chinese conform to the MRC hypothesis. However, it is also observed that though most verbs fall into only one ontological type as either a manner or a result verb, some verbs do exhibit dual ways of categorization, i.e. they can be both manner and result verbs. For example, the verbs 走 zǒu "walk", 跑 pǎo "run" and 飞 fēi "fly" in Modern Chinese can be either manner or result verbs. In Old Chinese, the verb 走 zǒu "run" can also be used as a manner and result verb. The questions are why these verbs demonstrate the dual ways of categorization and what are the possible factors affecting their distinct lexicalization patterns. Focusing on the three verbs with distinct lexicalization patterns, 走 zǒu "run/walk", 跑 pǎo "run" and 飞 fēi "fly", I will look at their lexical semantics and grammatical behaviors from a diachronic perspective aiming at finding the possible factors affecting their distinct lexicalization patterns and further revealing the relation between lexical semantics and syntactic structures.

With an analysis based on the actual uses of the three verbs in the corpora of Chinese texts from the Old Chinese period to the Modern Chinese period, I argue that the directed motion sense of these manner verbs mainly derives from pragmatic inference from the contexts and cognitive preference for the conceptualization of motion events. In addition, it is essential that favorable morphosyntactic constructions in the language promote the pragmatic sense to be lexicalized as the verb's lexical meaning. In other words, grammatical behaviors of motion verbs are not only determined by the conceptual component of verbs, but also affected by the morphosyntactic resources of the language. For example, as will be illustrated in the following section, the verb 走 zǒu "run/walk" is primarily a manner-of-motion verb, and with the help of contextual inference and cognitive preference for motion events, it has the potential to encode certain direction of motion, as it prototypically implies displacement of the figure. However, the specific direction encoded in the verb and its grammatical behaviors are not fully determined by the lexical semantics of the verb itself. The grammatical constructions available in the language also account for the evolution of its lexical semantics and grammatical behaviors.

This chapter starts with a survey of semantic and syntactic evolution of motion verbs. Then I will try to explore the possible factors affecting their distinct ways of evolution. In Old Chinese period, the uses of the three verbs are based on attested examples in three books,《左传》,《韩非子》, and《史记》. In Middle Chinese period, four books are looked up, which are《世说新语》,《百喻经》,《祖堂集》, and《敦煌变文》. In Pre-modern Chinese period, besides《朴通事谚解》,《老乞大谚解》,《儒林外史》,《红楼梦》, and《儿女英雄传》which are selected to examine directly, the indirect statistic data concerning the uses of the verbs collected by Bai (2007) from texts based on sub-periodization of Pre-modern Chinese period corresponding to alternations of dynasties are also made reference to. The data in Modern Chinese are mainly from the corpus of Modern Chinese constructed by the Center for Chinese Linguistics at Peking University.

5.1 The Evolution of Motion Verbs in Their Lexical Semantics and Grammatical Behaviors

In Modern Chinese, the three verbs 走 zǒu "walk", 跑 pǎo "run" and 飞 fēi "fly" are grouped together because they show similar lexicalization patterns. Based on the discussion in Chapter 3, as polysemous motion verbs, they are the only three verbs which may lexicalize both the manner and direction of motion. Moreover, in their directed motion sense, they indicate the same direction of motion "departure from a reference object". However, it does not entail the three verbs have also undergone the same evolution process in their lexical semantics and grammatical behaviors from Old to Modern Chinese period. In fact, the three verbs not only contrast with each other as to the specific period in which they enter Chinese lexicon but also have different lexicalization patterns in each synchronic period of Chinese language. Thus it is more convenient and plausible to trace the evolution processes of the three verbs separately. I will start with the verb 走 zǒu "run/walk" and then turn to 跑 pǎo "run" and 飞 fēi "fly" in sequence.

5.1.1 走 zǒu "walk/run"

Along the diachronic evolution from Old to Modern Chinese, the verb 走 zǒu "run/walk" has kept its polysemous nature constant, i.e. in both periods, it can be either a manner or a result verb. However, its grammatical behaviors and lexicalization patterns in the two periods are different.

In Old Chinese 走 zǒu "run/walk" is primarily a manner-of-motion verb specifying prototypically human being's way of motion: using legs to move quickly, as shown in (118). As I have illustrated in Chapter 4 when it is used as a manner-of-motion verb, it shows the grammatical property of manner verbs in the way that it does not specify the direction of motion and thus compatible with verbs expressing varied directions.

(118) 啬夫　　　　　馳，　庶人　　　走。(《左传》)
　　　 sèfū　　　　　chí　shùrén　　　zǒu
　　　 lower.ranking.officers gallop common.people **run**
　　　 "The lower ranking officers galloped and the common people ran about."

In addition, it can also be used as a directed motion verb, since followed by noun phrases immediately as reference objects it can lexicalize the goal of motion, as in (119). Nevertheless, in this case it doesn't violate the MRC hypothesis, since when it is used in the directed motion sense it has changed its ontological type from a manner verb to a directed motion one through tone alternation.

(119) 奉 君　　　以　　　走　　固宫 (《左传》)

　　　fèng jūn　　yǐ　　zǒu　Gùgōng

　　　serve the king CONJ **run　Gu Palace**

　　　"serve the king to run to Gu Palace"

走 zǒu "walk" is also polysemous in Modern Chinese, but both the lexicalized meaning components and grammatical behaviors are different from its ancestor. To be specific, the lexicalized manner sense of the verb is not "run" any more; rather it has been changed into "walk". In addition, the directed motion sense has also evolved from a goal-oriented path "go to" to a source-oriented path "departing from a reference object". This change can be attested by the contrast between (119) and (120). In (119) above, the noun phrase Gùgōng "Gu Palace" is the goal of the motion, but (120) below describes a situation that a balloon flew away from a reference object, and thus the direction 走 zǒu "walk" indicates is the source of the motion "departure from a reference object".

(120) 气球　　飘　　走　　了。

　　　qìqiú　piāo zǒu　le

　　　balloon **float　walk** ASP

　　　"The balloon flew away."

The grammatical behaviors of the verb in two periods also form a clear contrast: Whereas it can be followed immediately by noun phrases as reference objects of the motion in Old Chinese as in (119), it cannot appear in this kind of constructions in Modern Chinese. Then the questions are the following: When and how the verb has changed its lexicalized meaning components and grammatical behaviors? Are these changes accidental or affected by certain factors in a systematic way? Can all these changes be explained simply by the lexical semantics of the verb itself?

To answer these questions, I first make comparison between the uses of the verb in Old Chinese period and Middle Chinese period to see whether there is certain evolution tendency which provides some clues for its change in lexical semantics and grammatical behaviors. I collect all the cases of its use as a motion verb in representative texts in both periods and then pick up the cases in which it is used as a goal-oriented path verb "go to", i.e. when it is followed directly by noun phrases. The percentages of its use as a directed motion verb are calculated in both periods. The result is shown in Table 4.

Table 4 The Evolution of the Grammatical Behaviors of 走 zǒu "run" from Old to Middle Chinese

Period. Texts	No. of Occurrence			
	Total Number		"go to" 走 zou "run" + G	
Old Chinese	《左传》	37	484 (100%)	10	177 (37%)
	《韩非子》	50		9	
	《史记》	397		158	
Middle Chinese	《世说新语》	11	211 (100%)	1	7 (3%)
	《百喻经》	10		0	
	《祖堂集》	33		0	
	《敦煌变文》	157		6	

As shown in Table 4, there is no doubt that the verb 走 zǒu "run" is dominantly used in its manner sense, as in both periods the percentages of its directed motion sense are less than 40%. This confirms that the manner sense is its primary meaning. However, though its directed motion sense only takes a small percentage of all of its uses, the tendency related to the change in its lexical semantics can also be attested in the table. Its uses in the directed motion sense "go to" in Old Chinese period takes 37% of all its uses as a motion verb, but in Middle Chinese period the goal-oriented path sense drops to only 3%. This means that the goal-oriented path sense of 走 zǒu "run" is most often used in Old Chinese period, and it has greatly declined in Middle Chinese period. This tendency is also observed in Ma (2008). In her study, she also selects texts from Old to Middle Chinese period and found that 走 zǒu "run" is less often followed by noun phrases directly in Middle Chinese period. However, in her study the decrease seems to be less obvious. The reason for the discrepancy is probably due to different writing styles the chosen texts represent. Texts using Classical Chinese literary language are more likely to follow the writing style in Old Chinese period. As the selected texts in Middle Chinese period in present study are more closely connected to spoken language of the period, they in particular represent the new evolutionary trend of Chinese language.

Then the question is along the decline of the goal-oriented path sense of 走 zǒu "run" whether the directed motion sense used in Modern Chinese "depart from a reference object" also appears at the same time. The data show that it is not the case, since in Middle Chinese period there is hardly any case where the verb is used in the source-oriented path sense. The source-oriented path sense probably appears later. In order to better understand the evolutionary tendency of the lexical semantics of 走 zǒu "run", the Pre-modern Chinese period is subdivided according to the periodization based on the alternations of dynasties and the uses of the verb in representative texts in different dynasties are compared. With respect to all of its uses as a motion verb, the percentages of the source-oriented path sense in representative texts in four different dynasties are calculated. The result is shown in Table 5.

Table 5 The Use of 走 zǒu "run/walk" in Source-Oriented Path Sense in Pre-modern Chinese Period

Pre-modern Chinese	No. of Occurrence	
	Total number	"Depart from a reference object"
Sòng, Liáo, Jīn	825	2 (0.2%)
Yuán	131	13 (10%)
Míng	422	44 (11%)
Qīng	469	109 (23%)

It can be seen from Table 5 that at the beginning of Pre-modern Chinese, there is rarely any case of its use in the source-oriented path sense "depart from a reference object". It provides evidence that the source-oriented path sense does not seem to be lexicalized in the verb until Pre-modern Chinese period. Though the percentage of its use in the source-oriented path sense is still relatively low in the Yuan and Ming dynasties, it increases gradually. Approaching the end of Pre-modern Chinese period, the percentage increases to 22%.

The data indicate that though from Pre-modern Chinese period the manner sense is still the dominant sense of 走 zǒu "walk", but when used as a directed motion verb, the sense of "depart from a reference object" gradually gains currency in the place of the goal direction meaning. This tendency is also observed by Bai (2007), Zhang (2005), etc. Bai analyzes the distribution of varied senses of 走 zǒu "walk" in Middle and Pre-modern Chinese periods and found that the sense of "go to" completely disappeared in spoken language in the Song Dynasty (the beginning of Pre-modern Chinese period), and in contrast in the Ming Dynasty the directed motion sense of "depart from a reference object" has become the common sense of the verb. However, the grammatical behavior of 走 zǒu "walk" is still quite different from Modern Chinese, as then it is commonly used as the bare verb to encode the direction, and it often depends on the context to differentiate the directed motion sense from its manner sense.

It has been uncovered so far that the verb 走 zǒu "run/walk" has been dominantly used as a manner-of-motion verb throughout its evolution from Old to Modern Chinese, but its directed motion sense has changed in the process. Its goal-oriented path sense "go to" was most often used in Old Chinese period, but from Middle Chinese period it greatly declined. From Pre-modern Chinese period, another directed motion sense "depart from a reference object" has gradually been used. The verb 飞 fēi "fly" will be looked at in next section.

5.1.2　飞 fēi "fly"

The verb 飞 fēi "fly" also enters Chinese lexicon before Old Chinese period, but its evolution line is quite different from 走 zǒu "run/walk". Compared with 走

zǒu "run/walk", 飞 fēi "fly" is not a motion verb with high frequency of occurrence in texts of Old Chinese period. There are only 28 cases of its use as a motion verb in《左传》,《韩非子》, and《史记》. No use of this verb is found in《论语》and《孟子》. Looking up all these cases, I find that the verb is only used as a manner verb specifying the manner of motion as "fly", which can be literally understood as "to move through air (using wings)". As to its grammatical behavior, 飞 fēi "fly" is not found to be immediately followed by any noun phrases in Old Chinese. Thus different from the verb 走 zǒu "run/walk", it cannot specify the goal of the motion. That is, 飞 fēi "fly" is not polysemous in Old Chinese, since it does not have a separate directed motion sense. Two examples of its use as manner verbs in Old Chinese period are given in (121).

(121) a. 有　鸮　飞　入　贾　生　　舍，　　止　于　坐　隅。

(《史记》)

yǒu　xiāo **fēi** rù　　Jiǎ Shēng shè　zhǐ yú　zuò yú

have owl **fly** **enter** Jia　Sheng　house stop at　seat corner

"An owl flew to Jia Sheng's house and stopped at the corner of a seat."

b. 六　鹢　退　　　　　飞　过　宋　　都。(《左传》)

liù　yì　tuì　　　　　**fēi guò** Sòng dū

six　fish hawk backward **fly pass** Song capital

"Six fish hawks flew backwards and passed the capital of Song."

In the two example sentences the themes of the movements specified by 飞 fēi "fly" are both birds. In (121)a it forms a serial verb construction with a path verb 入 rù "enter". It also appears with two path verbs 退 tuì "backward" and 过 guò "pass" in (121)b. Both sentences indicate that the verb 飞 fēi "fly" itself does not specify the direction of motion and it is a pure manner verb.

However, interestingly enough, checking its use in Middle Chinese, I do find several cases in which 飞 fēi "fly" are used to be followed by noun phrases to specify the goal of motion, as in (122). In the sentence, 飞 fēi "fly" is directly followed by a noun 空 kōng "sky" which indicates the goal of the motion.

(122) 或　　　　有 飞 空 罗汉······ (《敦煌变文》)
　　　 huò　　　 yǒu fēi kōng luóhàn
　　　 sometimes have **fly sky** arhat
　　　 "Sometimes there are arhats flying to the sky..."

The fact that 飞 fēi "fly" can be used in this way is quite surprising because it is just contrary to the evolution tendency of the grammatical behavior of 走 zǒu "run/walk", whose directed motion sense "go to" has been greatly weaken in Middle Chinese period. What is more puzzling is that even in Old Chinese period when other manner-of-motion verbs such as 走 zǒu "run", 趋 qū "hurry up", 奔 bēn "run", etc., are more likely to be followed by noun phrases indicating the goal of motion, the verb 飞 fēi "fly" cannot be used in the same way. Then why it can be used in this construction in Middle Chinese period deserves explanation. I will come back to it in Section 5.2.2.

5.1.3 跑 pǎo "run"

In contrast with the other two verbs discussed above, 跑 pǎo "run" enters Chinese lexicon much later, and the first cases of its use are found in the texts composed in the Pre-modern Chinese period (Wang, 1980). There is also a consensus among scholars that the original meaning of 跑 pǎo "run" is to indicate the action that animals such as tigers use claws to dig the ground (Wang, 1980). Because the manner in which animals use claws to dig ground is similar to the manner of running, after entering the lexicon, 跑 pǎo "run" gradually acquires the manner of motion sense "run". Its use as a motion verb becomes common in the Ming Dynasty, the later part of Pre-modern Chinese period. More importantly, because 跑 pǎo "run" and 走 zǒu "run" encode the similar manner of motion, 跑 pǎo "run" gradually replaces the manner use of 走 zǒu "run", which correspondingly drops the manner sense "run" and develops its new manner sense "walk" gradually. As 跑 pǎo "run" replaces the manner use of 走 zǒu "run/walk", it is expected that it also inherits the grammatical behaviors of 走 zǒu "run/walk". For example, it should be reasonable if it could also be followed by noun phrases to indicate the goal of motion. However, it is not the case, because it is not found in constructions where it is followed by noun phrases encoding the goal of motion. Then the question is why 跑 pǎo "run" only inherits the manner sense of 走 zǒu "run/walk", but shows distinct grammatical behaviors. It will also be explained in Section 5.2.2.

To summarize, though the three verbs are all polysemous in Modern Chinese, they have gone through different evolution processes, which are represented in Figure 1.

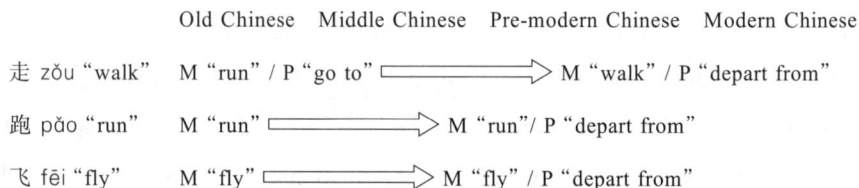

Old Chinese   Middle Chinese   Pre-modern Chinese   Modern Chinese

走 zǒu "walk"   M "run" / P "go to" ⟹ M "walk" / P "depart from"

跑 pǎo "run"   M "run" ⟹ M "run"/ P "depart from"

飞 fēi "fly"   M "fly" ⟹ M "fly" / P "depart from"

Figure 1 The Evolution Processes of 走 zǒu "run/walk", 跑 pǎo "run" and 飞 fēi "fly"

As can be seen in Figure 1, 走 zǒu "run/walk" and 飞 fēi "fly" enter Chinese lexicon before Old Chinese period, but only 走 zǒu "run/walk" is polysemous in Old Chinese, encoding either manner sense "run" or path sense "go to". 飞 fēi "fly" is only used as a manner verb till Pre-modern Chinese period. However, approaching Pre-modern Chinese, the manner and the path sense of 走 zǒu "run/walk" have evolved into "walk" and "depart from a reference object" respectively. Inheriting the manner sense of 走 zǒu "run/walk" in Old Chinese, 跑 pǎo "run" starts to be used as a motion verb much later, i.e. in Pre-modern Chinese period, but it cannot encode the same goal direction as 走 zǒu "run/walk" throughout its semantic evolution. Based on the evolution processes of the three verbs, I will try to explore the possible factors affecting their distinct evolution processes and to further reveal the relation between the lexicon and syntactic structures.

5.2 Factors Affecting the Change of the Lexicalization Patterns of Motion Verbs

With regard to the diachronic evolution of these verbs, in this part, I will try to analyze factors which may contribute to their lexicalization patterns in certain synchronic period and their diachronic development. As illustrated in Section 5.1 that the lexicalization patterns of the three verbs are not entirely consistent, my analysis will firstly focus on the verb 走 zǒu "run/walk", since it shows the most distinct lexical meaning and the greatest variable behaviors through the evolution of Chinese language. Then with reference to the factors identified to affecting the lexicalization patterns of 走 zǒu "run/walk", I will discuss 飞 fēi "fly" and 跑 pǎo "run" to explore the possible reasons for their unique ways of lexicalization patterns.

5.2.1 Possible Factors Affecting the Evolution of the Lexicalization Patterns of 走 zǒu "walk/run"

5.2.1.1 Pragmatic Inference and Cognitive Preference

Though from Old to Modern Chinese, 走 zǒu "run/walk" is dominantly used as a manner-of-motion verb, its manner sense has changed from "run" to "walk". It's interesting that in spite of its different lexicalized manners in Old and Modern Chinese, the verb has developed a separate directed motion sense in both periods. Based on my analysis of its actual uses in the corpus, I will show that the emergence of its lexicalized directional sense is partly due to the pragmatic inference and cognitive preference related to the nature of motion event specified by the verb. Pragmatic inference related to a common core of manner-of-motion verbs such as run and walk shared by most languages promotes the emergence of its directional sense. Goal-biased cognitive preference in conceptualizing motion events can also partly explain the specific direction it encodes at different synchronic periods.

It is observed that manner-of-motion verbs have varied preference for directional interpretation (Bouchard, 1995; Nikitina, 2008). In spite of different lexicalization patterns related to language typology, manner verbs favoring directional interpretation seem to cluster together across languages. Levin et al. (2009) suggest a pragmatic account that directional interpretation of manner verbs can be explained by pragmatic factors such as the nature of the manner, aspect and ground/path properties related to motion events. Cross-linguistically manner-of-motion verbs which convey simpler and less elaborated manners are more likely to have directional interpretations than other ones. Verbs that describe shorter events than verbs describe a process with a greater duration are more ready to express displacement.

As to the nature of manner encoded in 走 zǒu "run/walk", it fits the feature of the type of verbs favoring directional reading. The two possible manners encoded in 走 zǒu "run/walk" in Old and Modern Chinese, "run" and "walk", though different, are both major gaits of human's motion and reflect the human beings' conceptual structure of world (Malt et al., 2008). Like their counterparts in English, they are more likely to convey displacement, favoring a directional reading even without help of other path-indicating elements in a sentence. According to Rappaport Hovav and Levin (2015), though as to the lexical entailment, these verbs do not entail the path of motion, they lexicalize a manner that strongly suggests the displacement of an entity; they are what Talmy (2000) calls "implied fulfillment verbs". In this sense, they are different from manner-of-motion verbs like stomp and *dance* in English, which without help of other direction indicating elements, are unlikely to covey a directional sense. For example, as shown in (123), with run or walk as the main verb of the sentence, displacement of the figure is favored in (123a), but the figure's in-place action is preferred if the main verb is replaced by stomp or dance in (123b).

> (123) a. He ran/walked. (displacement favored)
>
> b. He stomped/danced. (in-place action favored)

This observation can also be confirmed when two different types of manner-of-motion verbs co-occur with locative prepositions. Though with proper contextual support, all manner-of-motion verbs in English can have directional interpretation, when followed by a locative prepositional phrase "in the room", run and walk are more ready to have directional interpretation than stomp and dance, as shown in (124).

(124) a. John ran/walked in the room.

b. John stomped/danced in the room.

Moreover, there is also cross-linguistic evidence for this observation. In Japanese, verbs like aruku "walk" and hashiru "run" are called path-oriented manner-of-motion verbs (Kitahara, 2009), because in certain constructions (e. g. causative constructions) these verbs may co-occur with ni-phrases to indicate the direction of motion, as seen in (125). To be sure, as explained by these researchers (Ono, 2010; Usuki, 2011; Namiki, 2012) for these verbs to have a directional reading some other factors are also at work, but the type of manner verbs are obviously restricted to these path-oriented verbs.

(125) a. Nobita-ga Jaian-o ichirui-ni hashir-ase-ta.

Nobita-NOM Jaian-ACC first-to run-ASE-PAST

"Nobita caused Jaian to run to first."

(Ono, 2010: 117)

b. Iwakuma-ga Omatsu-o ichirui-ni aruk-ase-ta.

Iwakuma-NOM Omatsu-ACC first-to walk-ASE-PAST

"Iwakuma caused Omatsu to walk to first."

(Usuki, 2011: 3)

Similar situations have also been found in Spanish and Italian. Under favorable pragmatic contexts, verbs specifying similar manners of motion in Spanish such as volar "fly", correr "run", and caminar "walk" as well as in Italian such as correre "run", saltare "jump", and volare "fly" are more likely to have directional interpretations than other manner-of-motion verbs. (Folli, Ramchand, 2005; Levin et al., 2009). Cross-linguistic language acquisition also proves that these verbs belong to a subtype of manner-of-motion verbs which are inherent to displacement to a goal. The natures of manner they describe are characteristic of animate entities moving along with a goal to reach (Allen et al., 2007; Levin et al., 2009). In fact manners specified in the three motion verbs 走 zǒu "run/walk", 跑 pǎo "run" and 飞 fēi "fly" in Chinese generally fall into the subtype of manner-of-motion verbs which prefer directional interpretation cross-linguistically. Therefore, strongly inferred directional interpretation from these verbs facilitates their lexicalization of the path sense.

However another fact concerning the directional sense of 走 zǒu "run" also needs to be noted, i.e. when it is used in the directional sense in Old Chinese, it always specifies a goal direction "go to". As shown in (126), the noun phrases following 走 zǒu "run" always indicate the goal of the motion.

(126) a. 齐侯　驾，　　　将　走　游棠。(《左传》)
　　　 Qí hóu jià　　　 jiāng zǒu Yóutáng
　　　 Qi Duke ride.chariot will **run Youtang**
　　　 "The Duke of Qi rode a chariot and wanted to run to Youtang."

 b. 百濮　离　　居，将　各　走　其邑。(《左传》)
　 Bǎipú lí　　 jū jiāng gè　 zǒu qí yì
　 Baipu scattered live will each **run his town**
　 "People of Baipu live in scattered communities and they would go back to their own town."

In (126), the two locative nouns 游棠 Yóutáng "Youtang" and 邑 yì "town" following 走 zǒu "run" both unambiguously indicate the goal of the motion.

Then one may wonder even though the nature of the verb and other semantic features of the motion events support a pragmatic inference of the directional reading of the verb, why the verb encodes the goal rather than the source or other types of path schema and where the specific directional interpretation "go to" comes from. Results from recent research on spatial semantics may help explain the puzzling problem. It has been demonstrated that there is a goal-bias cognitive preference in language. That is, the endpoint of motion receives asymmetrical emphasis over the starting point or source of motion in terms of semantic and syntactic representation. (Ikegami, 1987; Lakusta, Landau, 2005; Papafrgou, 2010; Kabata, 2013) This cognitive preference is reflected in both language structure and language use. As to language structure, goal-oriented paths tend to be unmarked in languages, whereas source-oriented paths tend to be marked (Fillmore, 1997; Ihara, Fujita, 2000; Jackendoff, 1983). For example, in many languages, unmarked and stative places are more ready to be interpreted as a goal-oriented path, but not a source-oriented path. Fillmore (1997) notes that in the sentence "The cat ran behind the sofa.", the complement "behind the sofa" can be used either as a non-directional locative place complement, or as a goal path complement, so the sentence is ambiguous in the way that it may have a goal-oriented directional motion reading "the cat ran to a place behind the sofa" or a in-place action reading "the cat ran in a place behind the sofa". However, it can never mean "the cat ran from behind the sofa". Concerning language use, it is reported that goal paths are mentioned more often than source paths (Lakusta, Landau, 2012). Concerning to language use, Papafragou (2010) and Lakusta and Landau (2012) observe that goal configuration changes are detected more accurately than other path information in language comprehension. In language production tasks, goal objects are also referred to more frequently by speakers.

In Old Chinese the goal direction specified by 走 zǒu "run" is partly motivated by the goal-biased cognitive preference. As a verb-framed language dominantly rendering the path schema into verbs, Old Chinese has a large path lexicon. More importantly, many of the path verbs describe goal-salient path schema and they require the goal arguments to be overtly expressed. Thus the most common syntactic structure these path verbs are used in is that they are followed immediately by noun phrases indicating the goal of the motion. For example, goal-salient path verbs in Old Chinese such as 如 rú "go to", 适 shì "go to", 之 zhī "go to", 造 zào "arrive", etc., all require the goal object to be expressed, as shown in (127).

(127) a. 郑伯　　如　周，　始　　朝

Zhèngbó rú Zhōu shǐ cháo

Zhengbo **go.to Zhou** begin have.an.audience.with

桓　　王　　　　也。(《左传》)

Huán wáng yě

Huang Lord AFFIR. PART

"Zhengbo went to Zhou and began to have an audience with the Lord Huan."

b. 孔子　　适　周，　将　问　礼　与　老子。

(《史记》)

Kǒngzǐ **shì Zhōu** jiāng wèn lǐ yǔ Lǎozǐ

Confucius **go.to Zhou** will ask rites to Laozi

"Confucius went to Zhou and wanted to ask Laozi about rites."

c. 大夫　　仇牧　闻　之，以　兵

dàfū Qiú Mù wén zhī yǐ bīng

grand.master Qiu Mu hear it with weapons

造　公门。(《史记》)

zào gōng mén

arrive gate.of.the.lord's.residence

"Grand Master Qiu Mu heard it and went to the gate of the lord's residence with weapons."

The prevalence of goal-salient path verbs in Old Chinese and the corresponding syntactic structure in which they typically appear are the evidence that goal-biased cognitive preference is represented in the lexical semantics of verb lexicon in Old Chinese on the one hand, and on the other hand they also provide appropriate construction templates for the originally direction-neutral verbs to build goal direction inference.

Nevertheless, in Modern Chinese goal-biased cognitive preference is not reflected through the lexicalization of path in verbs any more; rather it is reflected through finer-grained goal indicating directional complements such as 进 jìn "enter", 回 huí "return", 到 dào "arrive", 上 shàng "ascend", etc., since the dominant framing type of motion events has been changed from verb-framed to satellite-framed type. The goal direction lexicalized in 走 zǒu "run" gives way to specialized directional complements. As a result of the interaction between displacement-favored conceptual components in 走 zǒu "run/walk" and the property of directional verbal compound construction, it instead encodes another directed motion sense "depart from a reference object". It will be further illustrated in Section 5.2.1.2.

5.2.1.2 The Change in Motion Event Framing Type and Morphosyntactic Structure

Though the pragmatic inference and the cognitive preference are important factors contributing to lexicalization patterns of motion verbs, these factors alone cannot completely explain the distinct lexicalization patterns of the verb 走 zǒu "run/walk". The actual lexicalization of certain sense of the verb is also affected by morphosyntactic structure available in the language. As shown in Section 5.1, along with the evolution of Chinese language, the lexicalized direction sense of 走 zǒu "run/walk" has not been kept unchanged. Approaching the Middle Chinese period, its lexicalized direction "go to" in Old Chinese has greatly weakened and has virtually disappeared in Pre-modern Chinese period. Instead, another directed motion sense "depart from a reference object" has been gradually lexicalized and consolidated. This line of evolution cannot be completely explained only with the help of pragmatic and cognitive factors, since the conceptual components related to the verb haven't changed much. In fact, it is also a result of the two-way interaction between the verb's conceptual components and morphosyntactic structure available in Chinese. The arising and decline of goal path sense encoded in 走 zǒu "run/walk" is closely related to the availability of relevant morphosyntactic resources in certain synchronic period of Chinese language. This point can be seen from two perspectives.

First, as to motion event framing, the typical syntactic devices used to encode path schema affect the emergence and decline of the directed motion sense of 走 zǒu "run/walk". In Old Chinese period, Chinese is argued to be a verb-framed language, which dominantly renders the core schema path into verbs (Shi, Wu, 2014). The syntactic structure "path verb + goal object", which is used to encode goal path, provides an ideal construction template for manner verbs like 走 zǒu "run" to enter the schematic slot of "path verb" and acquire the directed motion sense "go to", analogical to other goal-bound path verbs. Thus it's natural that it can encode the goal-oriented direction in Old Chinese.

However, from Middle to Pre-modern Chinese period, the framing type of the language has gradually evolved from verb-framed to satellite-framed, and the goal paths are more likely to be rendered into directional complements rather than main verbs. As a result of this typological shift, without overtly represented direction-indicating elements, manner verbs cannot encode goal paths any more. It explains the gradual decline of the directed motion sense encoded in 走 zǒu "run" from Middle to Pre-modern Chinese period.

From Pre-modern to Modern Chinese period, when the directional verbal compound (DVC) becomes the dominant syntactic structure to encode motion events, besides the core members of directional complements such as 进 jìn "enter", 回 huí "return", 到 dào "arrive", 上 shàng "ascend", etc., other less-prototypical verbs are also attracted to be used as satellites in DVCs. Since the conceptual component of 走 zǒu "walk" is also compatible with displacement interpretation, it becomes one of the newly developed candidates as directional complements in DVCs lexicalizing the directed motion sense, though it needs to be noted that at this time the specific direction encoded in 走 zǒu "walk" has become "depart from a reference object". The evidence that shows this evolution process is attested in Lamarre (2013). In her study, Lamarre analyzes the use of 走 zǒu "walk" as a directional complement from Pre-modern to Modern Chinese period and reveals that both the number of occurrence and the range of verb types it may follow have increased. In Pre-modern Chinese period, to express the meaning of "depart from a reference object", the deictic verb 去 qù "go" is preferred to be used as a directional complement. The use of 走 zǒu "walk" is only restricted to a narrow range of verbs and the number of cases in this use is also found to fewer than that in Modern Chinese.

Second, the evolution of the directed motion sense of 走 zǒu "run/walk" is also affected by the change of phonological and morphological system of Chinese. In Old Chinese, phonological derivation process provides proper morphosyntactic devices for the lexicalization of directed motion in 走 zǒu "run". As discussed in Chapter 4, in Old Chinese related words are considered to have been derivable by changing the phonological properties of a base word (Pulleyblank, 1995). In particular, based on the most clearly documented phonological derivation process, derivation by tone alternation, a new sense or a new grammatical function of a verb, can be derived by changing the original tone into the departing tone. This kind of word derivational process makes it possible for a base verb to acquire a new sense or to change its categorical property without changing its written form. As to the derivation of path verbs from manner verbs in Old Chinese, the change concerning the verb's lexical semantics and grammatical behaviors can be conveniently marked by altering the tone of the manner verb. The derived path sense of the manner verb 走 zǒu "run" is just an example of this derivation process.

(128) a. 荀跞   掩   耳   而   走。(《左传》)

Xún Lì yǎn ěr ér   zǒu (ᶜtso)

Xun Li cover ears CONJ run

"Xun Li ran with his hands covering his ears."

b. 赵旃   弃   车   而   走   林……

(《左传》)

Zhào Zhān qì   chē er   zǒu (tsoˀ) lín

Zhao Zhan abandon cart CONJ run   forest

"Zhao Zhan abandoned his cart and ran to the forest..."

As shown in (128), when the original rising tone of 走 zǒu "run" ᶜtso[1] is

---

[1] As to the reconstruction of the pronunciation of Old Chinese words and the representation of the four tones refer to Section 4.1.1.

changed into departing tone tsoʾ, correspondingly the verb is changed into a path verb lexicalizing the goal direction of the motion. In fact, as attested by researchers (Wang, 2013; Sun, 1997), in Old Chinese the derivation of path verbs from manner verbs is not restricted to 走 zǒu "run", other manner verbs such as 趋 qū "hurry up", 奔 bēn "rush", 超 chāo "surpass", etc., also show this kind of lexicalization patterns, which demonstrates that the change in the semantic feature and grammatical category of verbs can be marked by altering phonological property in a systematic way. This kind of morphosyntactic resources in Old Chinese facilitates lexicalization of the goal-oriented path sense in the verb 走 zǒu "run".

However, from Middle to Modern Chinese periods, words in Chinese have undergone the processes of phonological simplification and disyllabification (e. g. Wang, 1980; Shi, 2002), which are also thought to have effect on the lexicalization patterns of motion verbs. In Middle Chinese period, phonological system greatly simplified and the phonological derivation system declined. As a consequence of the loss of this morphological inflection and complex tone system, the original contrastive pair of words which differentiates each other by phonological features cannot be distinguished and thus become homophones. Disyllabic words consequently arise within the language as a means of overcoming problems in communication caused by this proliferation of homophonous monosyllabic words (Lyu, 1963; Shi, 2002). For polysemous motion verbs encoding both the manner and result sense but differing each other only by tone properties like the verb 走 zǒu "run", the derived path sense is also suppressed for the same reason. Consistent with the disyllabification process, at the same period of time, the lexicalization patterns of path schema of motion events have gradually changed from verb-framed to satellite-framed with goal-indicating path verbs becoming disfavored in encoding the goal direction in motion events. This also promotes the decline of the goal-oriented path sense in 走 zǒu "run". Therefore, it can be seen that besides the conceptual components of verbs, the morphosyntactic structures do have effect on the possible lexicalizations of verbs. Both the emergence and decline of the goal sense of 走 zǒu "run/walk" are affected by the morphosyntactic structures available in certain synchronic period.

5.2.1.3 Grammaticalization of Directional Complements in DVCs

As discussed in the previous section, since Middle Chinese period the goal direction sense of 走 zǒu "run/walk" has gradually declined, and as to its grammatical behaviors it cannot be directly followed by locative nouns indicating the goal of the motion. Then it can be used either as a prototypical manner-of-motion verb followed by directional complements, in (129) or as a bare verb in a sentence like (130).

(129) a. 他　走　到　　金水　河　里。(《朴事通谚解》)
　　　　tā　zǒu　dào　Jīnshuǐ　Hé　lǐ
　　　　he　**walk arrive** Jinshui　River　LOC
　　　　"He walked to Jinshui River."

　　　b. 秦老　又　走　回　　家　去。(《儒林外史》)
　　　　Qínlǎo　yòu　zǒu huí　jiā　qù
　　　　Qinlao　again **walk return** home go
　　　　"Qinlao walked back home again."

(130) a. 那　妇人　便　走　了。(《朴事通谚解》)
　　　　nà　fùrén　biàn zǒu　le
　　　　that　woman then　**walk** ASP
　　　　"That woman then walked away."

　　　b. 范举人　先　走，屠户　和　邻居　都　跟　在　后面。
　　　　　　　　　　　　　　　　　　　　(《儒林外史》)
　　　　Fàn jǔrén　xiān zǒu　túhù　hé　línjū　dōu gēn zài hòumiàn
　　　　Fan Scholar first　**walk** butcher and neighbor all follow at backside
　　　　"Scholar Fan left first; the butcher and neighbors followed him
　　　at the back."

In the former case like (129), 走 zǒu "walk" co-occurs with directional complements expressing varied directions. In (129)a, it appears with another path verb 到 dào "arrive" which indicates the arrival of a goal object. In (129)b, the verb 回 huí "return" follows 走 zǒu "walk" to specify the direction of motion. 走 zǒu "walk" does not specify the direction of motion in either case, and this indicates that it is a pure manner-of-motion verb which does not specify any direction of motion in its lexical meaning.

However, in the latter case in (130), when it is used as a bare verb of the sentence, there is no overt path-indicating element to specify the accurate direction of motion. Since the goal direction is suppressed and the nature of manner encoded in 走 zǒu "walk" implies the displacement of the theme, when it is used in this way, another direction of motion, i.e. the source-oriented direction, becomes more salient. Thus pragmatically it may associate with a default direction "depart from a reference object". In fact, its source-oriented path sense just arises from the pragmatic meaning inferred from these cases. Sentences in (131) are also examples of this kind.

(131) a. 酒保　　见　开　了　门，撒手　便　走。

　　　　　　　　　　　　　　　　　　　　(《警世通言》)

　　　　jiǔbǎo　　jiàn　kāi　le　　mén sāshǒu biàn zǒu

　　　　bartender　see　open　ASP　door　let.go　then walk

　　　　"Seeing the door open, the bartender let go his hold and left."

b. 语　　毕，回身　　便　走。(《初刻拍案惊奇》)

　　yǔ　　bì　　huíshēn　biàn　zǒu

　　words　finish turn.around then　walk

　　"With these words, (they) turned around and left."

In the two example sentences in (131), 走 zǒu "walk" is used as a simple verb of the sentence. It is not followed by locative nouns nor does it appear with other path-indicating elements, so the direction of motion "depart from a reference object" just arises from the verbal semantics.

This observation is also supported by the corpus study by Bai (2007). She notes that in the texts of Pre-modern Chinese when used as the bare verb of a sentence, 走 zǒu "walk" can be interpreted as expressing either the manner "walk" or the path "depart from a reference object" sense, so it has to rely on the contextual information to determine what meaning it actually lexicalizes in a specific case. In other words, because the directed motion sense of 走 zǒu "walk" arises from its manner use, at the beginning of its lexicalization, the path meaning is still closely related to its manner sense; the motion of departing from a reference object is often carried out by human beings in a walking gait. Thus contextual information is essential to determine what sense it actually lexicalizes. She illustrates this with the use of the verb in Pre-modern Chinese texts. The two sentences in (132) are from《红楼梦》. The actual meaning of the same expression 快走 kuài zǒu "walk quickly" cannot be determined without the supporting contexts.

(132) a. 丫头……说:"老爷 回 来 了, 找 你 呢,
　　　　yātóu　shuō lǎoyé huí lái　le zhǎo nǐ　ne
　　　　maid　say　lord　return come ASP look.for you PART
　　　……快 　 走, 快 　 走。"
　　　　kuài　zǒu　kuài　zǒu
　　　　quickly walk quickly walk
　　　宝玉 听 了 只 得 跟 了 　出来。(《红楼梦》)
　　　Bǎoyù tīng le zhī dé gēn liǎo chū lái
　　　Bǎoyù hear ASP have.to follow　exit come
　　　"The maid … said, 'The master's back and wants you. Walk quickly. Hurry!' Hearing the words, Baoyu had to follow her out."

　 b. 贾瑞 …… 冰冷 　 打战
　　　Jiǎ Ruì …… bīnglěng dǎzhàn
　　　Jia Rui… icy.cold shutter

汉语位移动词中的方式结果互补性研究——共时与历时视角

| | | | | | | | | | | | The Manner/Result Complementarity in Chinese Motion Verbs: Synchronic and Diachronic Perspectives

只　见　贾蔷　　　跑　来　叫:"快　　走,　快　走!"

（《红楼梦》）

zhī　jiàn Jiǎ Qiáng pǎo lái　jiào **kuài**　**zǒu kuài zǒu**

only see　Jia Qiang　run　come call **quickly walk quickly walk**

"Jia Rui shivered with coldness and saw Jia Qiang running over calling, 'Quick! Get away!'"

In (132)a the sentence following 快走 kuài zǒu "walk quickly" indicates that 宝玉 Bǎoyù followed the maid out and did not go away, so the verb 走 zǒu "walk" is in its manner sense, but in (132)b 贾蔷 Jiǎ Qiáng called out to 贾瑞 Jiǎ Ruì and let him get away, so 走 zǒu "walk" is clearly in its directed motion sense meaning "depart from a reference object". However, without supporting information from the contexts, it is difficult to tell which sense the verb encodes when it is used as a bare verb of the sentence.

In Pre-modern Chinese period, the further interaction between the directed motion sense of 走 zǒu "walk", "depart from a reference object", and the construction meaning of directional verbal compounds lead to its grammaticalization as a source-oriented path morpheme. Before proceeding with this point, it is necessary to spend some time explaining the syntactic and semantic properties of the directional verbal compound (DVC) in Chinese. DVCs are a type of motion constructions in which two or three motion verbs are used together in adjacent positions with the second (and the third) one indicating the direction in which an entity moves as a result of action expressed by the first one. Because the direction in which an entity moves is also regarded as a kind of result, DVCs are generally considered as a subtype of resultative verbal compounds (RVCs), which are compounds consisting of two verbs with the second one indicating some result of the action or process conveyed by the first one (Li, Thompson, 1981). Though DVCs are different from RVCs in some aspects, they share major syntactic and semantic properties. First, they both tend to express bounded events. In a RVC, the second verb indicates the state the theme achieves, and in DVCs the second verb also marks the bound that the theme reaches or crosses in spatial relation. Second, DVCs like RVCs may form potential constructions by adding a negative potential marker 不 bù or a positive potential marker 得 de. Third, they are also one of the morphosyntactic strategies to express causative relations in Modern Chinese. As noted by scholars (e. g. Zhao, 2005) Modern Chinese does not have lexical and morphological causatives. Verbs which cannot express causative relations when used alone may be combined to form DVCs or RVCs to express caused motion or result. Verbs with lexical semantics compatible with the syntactic and semantic properties are more likely to be used in the two constructions. In fact, it is this compatibility between the lexical semantics of 走 zǒu "walk" and the DVC constructions that promotes the further consolidation of its source-oriented direction sense.

In Pre-modern Chinese, path verbs used in Old and Middle Chinese such as 上 shàng "ascend", 下 xià "descend", 进 jìn "enter", 回 huí "return", 过 guò "pass", 来 lái "come" and 去 qù "go" gradually grammaticalized into directional complements and followed an action verb they can form DVCs together. Among these directional complements, when used as V2 in DVC constructions, 来 lái "come" and 去 qù "go" express deictic path information with reference to the subjective deictic center, the speaker. Since the directed motion sense encoded in 走 zǒu "walk" is "depart from a reference object", it expresses similar path information as 去 qù "go", which indicates a path of "be away from the speaker". However, compared with 去 qù "go", 走 zǒu "walk" is more compatible with the DVC constructions and the use of 去 qù "go" has more restrictions. For example, when 去 qù "go" appears with self-agentive verbs, it generally cannot express bounded events. As noted by researchers (Liu, 1998; Lamarre, 2013), when 去 qù "go" follows self-agentive verbs such as 走 zǒu "walk", 跑 pǎo "run", 爬 pá "clamber", etc. it often co-occurs with adverbial phrases headed by prepositions such as 往 wǎng "toward", 向 xiàng "toward" and 朝 cháo "toward", which indicates that the motion events it describes are boundless. The fact that 去 qù "go" is unlikely to express bounded motion events is also attested by its compatibility with progressive time adverbial 正在 zhèngzài, as can be seen in (133).

汉语位移动词中的方式结果互补性研究——共时与历时视角

| | | | | | | | | | | | The Manner/Result Complementarity in Chinese Motion Verbs: Synchronic and Diachronic Perspectives

(133) 他 (正在)　　往　　　学校　　跑　去。

tā (zhèngzài)　wǎng　xuéxiào　pǎo　qù

he PROG　　towards school　run　go

"He is running towards school."

Different from the typical property of DVC, these verbal compounds with 去 qù "go" cannot form potential constructions either, as seen in (134).

(134) *跑/　　走/　爬　不　去

pǎo/　zǒu/　pá　bù　qù

run / walk/ crawl NEG go

"cannot run/walk/crawl away" (Intended meaning)

In addition, when 去 qù "go" follows some transitive verbs such as 摸 mō "feel", 投 tóu "cast", 看 kàn "look", etc., in DVCs, it cannot express caused-motion; rather it only expresses self-agentive motion, as illustrated in (135).

(135) 男孩子……向　　　李阿姨　床铺　　摸　去。

nánháizǐ　xiàng　Lǐ āyí　chuángpū　mō qù

boys　　towards Li aunt　bed　　　feel go

"Boys felt their way towards the bed of Aunt Li."

(Lamarre, 2013)

In (135), the verbal compound 摸去 mō qù "feel go" does not express a caused motion event in which some entity goes to somewhere described by V2 去 qù "go" as a result of the action specified by V1 摸 mō "feel"; rather it only expresses a self-agentive action that "boys felt their way towards the bed of Aunt Li". Thus, sometimes the caused motion cannot be expressed with the verb 去 qù "go" as the second verb of DVC.

In contrast, verbal compounds formed with 走 zǒu "walk" as V2 are more suitable to express motion events which demonstrate typical features of DVC constructions. They generally describe bounded motion events. For example, the two sentences in (136) form a contrast that the verbal compound formed with 走 zǒu "walk" as V2 in (136)a expresses a bounded motion event, but the verbal compound formed with 去 qù "go" as V2 in (136)b describes a boundless motion event, as the progressive time adverbial 正在 zhèngzài is compatible with 飞去 fēi qù "fly go", but not with 飞走 fēi zǒu "fly walk".

(136) a. 去 上海　　的　　　飞机 (*正在)　飞　走　了。
　　　　 qù Shànghǎi de　　 fēijī zhèngzài fēi zǒu le
　　　　 go Shanghai ASSOC plane PROG　　 fly walk ASP
　　　　 "The plane to Shanghai has flown away/is flying away."
　　　　 (Intended meaning)

b. 他看见　　两　 只 鸟　（正在）　 向　　右边　　飞去。
　 tā kànjiàn liǎng zhī niǎo zhèngzài xiàng yòu biān fēi qù
　 he see　　 two　 CL bird PROG　　 toward right side fly go
　 "He saw two birds fly to the right/ is flying to the right."

(Lamarre, 2013)

When 走 zǒu "walk" is used as V2, potential constructions can also be formed by inserting 不 bù and 得 de between V1 and 走 zǒu "walk", as in (137). In contrast, if V2 走 zǒu "walk" is replaced by 去 qù "go", the relevant potential constructions in (137) will sound very awkward, if not completely ungrammatical.

(137) a. 如果　你 还有　　其他 一些 东西　带　　不　走/去……
　　　　 rúguǒ nǐ háiyǒu qítā yīxiē dōngxī dài　 bù zǒu/qù
　　　　 if　　 you still have other some thing　 carry NEG walk/go
　　　　 "If you still have some other things that cannot be carried away…"

b. 大型　设备　和 货物　都 能　拉 得 走/去

dàxíng shèbèi　he huòwù dōu néng　lā de zǒu/qù

giant　equipment and cargo　all can　pull DE walk/go

"Giant equipment and cargos can all be pulled away."

Distinct from the syntactic distribution of 去 qù "go", DVCs formed with 走 zǒu "walk" as V2 also tend to express caused-motion events. Based on her analysis of DVCs formed with 走 zǒu "walk" as V2 in three novels in Modern Chinese period, Lamarre (2013) shows that 走 zǒu "walk" is often used following transitive verbs to describe caused-motion events. Zeng (2013) also compares the frequency of occurrence of 走 zǒu "walk" and 去 qù "go" when they follow 20 transitive verbs to form caused-motion events in a Chinese website (http://www.people.com. cn/) and demonstrates that for 12 of 20 verbs the token of 走 zǒu "walk" as V2 is far more than that of 去 qù "go" (the ration is more than 10:1). The tokens of 走 zǒu "walk" and 去 qù "go" used as V2 in these DVCs are shown in Table 6. Though there are 6 verbs which are more likely to select 去 qù "go" as V2 in DVC constructions, it is not surprising, because 走 zǒu "walk" and 去 qù "go" have distinct semantic focuses in that the former is source-oriented but the latter is goal-oriented, and the other goal profiling elements in sentences may prefer the use of 去 qù "go". For example, verbs used in V1 position such as 寄 jì "send", 捎 shāo "bring to" and 派 pài "send" prefer to co-occur with goal-oriented complements, so this kind of verbs selects 去 qù "go" more often than 走 zǒu "run/walk". In spite of this factor which affects the frequency of occurrence of the two verbs, Zeng summarizes that 走 zǒu "walk" is more suitable to express caused-motion events.

Table 6　The Frequency of Occurrence of V+去 qù "go" and V+走 zǒu "walk" as V2 in Causative Motion Events in Modern Chinese

V	V+去 qù	V+走 zǒu	V	V+去 qù	V+走 zǒu
拿 ná "hold"	4795	8532	借 jiè "borrow"	194	325
带 dài "carry"	7969	19495	抢 qiǎng "rob"	1266	7810

Continued

V	V+去 qù	V+走 zǒu	V	V+去 qù	V+走 zǒu
抬 tái "lift up"	33	387	偷 tōu "steal"	355	3125
抱 bào "embrace"	58	713	调 diào "transfer"	604	1287
运 yùn "transport"	342	2319	送 sòng "deliver"	15670	4263
拉 lā "pull"	789	2174	寄 jì "post"	1485	57
端 duān "carry"	75	195	捎 shāo "bring to"	386	12
取 qǔ "take"	85	2577	叫 jiào "bid"	932	213
买 mǎi "buy"	571	3015	请 qǐng "invite"	900	276
抓 zhuā "grasp"	586	1453	派 pài "send"	1580	20

(Zeng, 2013)

Furthermore, when 走 zǒu "walk" is used as V2 in DVCs, it is more compatible with the 把 BA and 被 BEI constructions, since these two constructions also generally require their predicates to be bounded. Lambarre (2013) analyzes the synchronic and diachronic evolution of V+走 zǒu "walk" and found that in Modern Chinese among all the uses of V+走 zǒu "walk", most cases are used in 把 BA and 被 BEI constructions. In addition, from a diachronic perspective from Pre-modern to Modern Chinese period, 走 zǒu "walk" is used to express caused-motion events in 把 BA and 被 BEI constructions with an increasing rate and has gradually replaced 去 qù "go". Lamarre concludes that it is the evidence that 走 zǒu "walk" becomes more grammaticalized as a result of the interaction between its lexical semantics and relevant construction meaning.

To summarize, the factors affecting the evolution processes of the lexicalization patterns of 走 zǒu "run/walk" can be represented as Figure 2.

Old / Middle Chinese   Pre-modern Chinese / Modern Chinese

"go to"
GOAL
(P)

←   pragmatic inference
DISPLACEMENT   →

"depart from"
SOURCE
(P)

(M)

"run" → "walk"

走 zǒu "run/walk"

goal-biased preference
derivation by tone alternation
V-framed type

suppression of goal
disyllabification
S-framed type
DVC construction

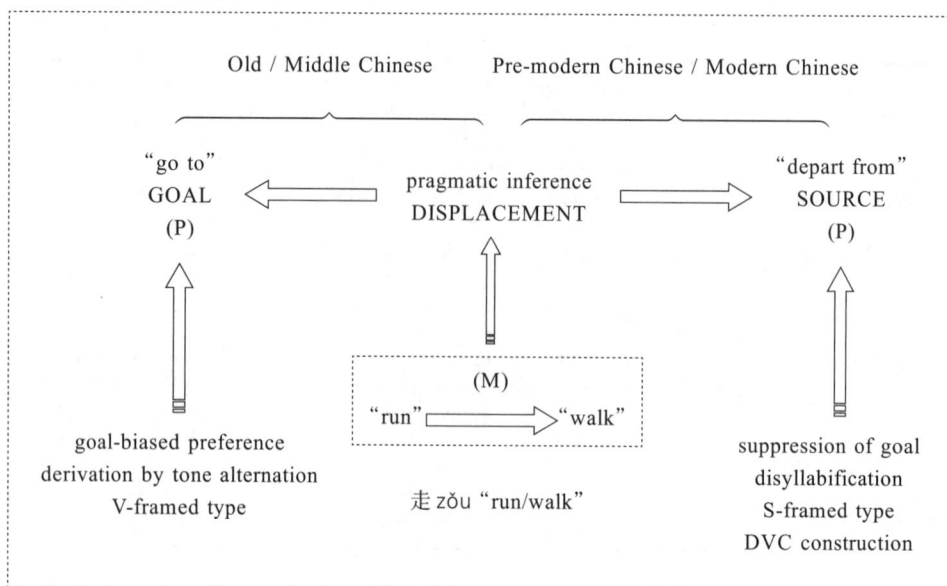

Figure 2   The Factors Affecting the Lexical Evolution of 走 zǒu "run/walk"

In this figure, the arrow in the small dotted square represents the diachronic lexical evolution of the manner sense of 走 zǒu "run/walk", i.e. its manner sense evolves from "run" to "walk". The whole big dotted square represents the evolution of its directed motion sense and relevant factors affecting the lexicalization of the specific sense. The plain arrows indicate the process of the actual lexicalization of certain sense. The arrows with dotted tails illustrate the relevant factors which are assumed to affect the lexicalization of certain sense. Generally, throughout the evolution process of 走 zǒu "run/walk" from Old to Modern Chinese, its distinct lexicalization patterns in each synchronic period result from the interaction between conceptual meaning components of the verb and the available morphosyntactic structures in certain developmental period of Chinese language. The nature of the manner encoded in 走 zǒu "run/walk" promotes the pragmatic inference of displacement, which is the basis for further lexicalization of the directional sense in both Old and Modern Chinese. However, the specific direction lexicalized in the verb, goal or source of the motion, is also affected by the morphosyntactic properties of the language. In Old Chinese, goal-biased cognitive preference reflected at the level of verb lexicon, verb-framed framing type of motion events and morphological derivation process by tone alternation promote the actual lexicalization of the goal-oriented direction. In Modern Chinese, the suppression of the goal path encoded at the level of verb lexicon, satellite-framed framing type of motion events, disyllabification of Chinese lexicon and the grammaticalization of directional complements in DVCs consolidate the lexicalization of the source-oriented direction.

5.2.2 Extending the Analysis of 飞 fēi "fly" and 跑 pǎo "run"

The lexicalization patterns of 飞 fēi "fly" and 跑 pǎo "run" can also be explained with reference to the factors which affect the diachronic evolution of the verb 走 zǒu "run/walk". As illustrated in Section 5.1.2, though 走 zǒu "run/walk", 飞 fēi "fly" and 跑 pǎo "run" are all polysemous encoding both manner and result senses in Modern Chinese, they do not show the same evolutionary line. 飞 fēi "fly" enters Chinese lexicon as a manner-of-motion verb before Old Chinese period, but different from 走 zǒu "run/walk", it does not develop a separate directed motion sense. 跑 pǎo "run" enters the lexicon much later and it is not attested to be used as a motion verb until Pre-modern Chinese period. In spite of the fact that 跑 pǎo "run" inherits the manner sense of 走 zǒu "run/walk" in Old Chinese, it does not develop the same directed motion sense "go to" as the verb 走 zǒu "run/walk" does. The derivation of their lexicalization patterns from 走 zǒu "run/walk" deserves explanations. To reveal the possible factors for their distinct evolutionary patterns I reexamine their actual uses in relevant corpus and find that the lack of the directed motion sense in 飞 fēi "fly" and 跑 pǎo "run" results from different factors: while the conceptual component encoded in 飞 fēi "fly" is unlikely to obtain an inferred goal direction sense in Old Chinese, there is no proper morphosyntactic structures available for 跑 pǎo "run" to lexicalize the goal path in Pre-modern Chinese period.

In Old Chinese, 走 zǒu "run/walk" and 飞 fēi "fly" are both basic motion verbs and can be conceptualized as an agent moving in certain manner. Though researchers (Rapapport Hovav, Levin, 1998; Pinker, 1989) consider a specific manner encoded in manner verbs as "idiosyncratic information" of the verb, which is opaque to the argument structure of the verb, the nature of the specific manner encoded in these verbs may affect their lexicalization patterns. Besides the specific details such as whether the relevant actions prototypically involve wings or legs, the manners encoded in the two verbs are different in a way that 走 zǒu "run/walk" is in particular used to describe motion events carried out by human being, but 飞 fēi "fly" is seldom used to describe human's motion in Old Chinese. I look up the use of 飞 fēi "fly" in《左传》,《韩非子》, and《史记》and found that the use of 飞 fēi "fly" is restricted to describing the manner of the motion of birds, phoenixes or dragons and no case is used to describe the motion of human beings. Two example sentences of its use are given in (138).

(138) a. 有　鸮　飞　入　贾　生　舍，　止　于　坐　隅。

《史记》

yǒu　xiāo fēi rù　Jiǎ Shēng shè　zhǐ yú zuò yú

have owl fly enter Jia Sheng house stop at seat corner

"An owl flew to Jia Sheng's house and stopped at the corner of a seat."

b. 六鹢　退　飞　过　宋　都。(《左传》)

liù yì　tuì　fēi guò Sòng　dū

six bird retreat fly pass Song.State capital

"Six birds flew past the capital of the State of Song in backward direction."

As human being's motion is more often than not characterized as intentional, it is easy to derivate a goal sense from manner-of-motion verbs describing intentional motion by human beings. In Old Chinese 飞 fēi "fly" is never conceptualized as an intentional or goal-bound motion event, so it is difficult to derivate a directed motion from its manner sense.

This point can also be supported by the grammatical behavior of 飞 fēi "fly" in Middle and Modern Chinese. As illustrated in Section 5.1, though 飞 fēi "fly" is not attested in the directed motion sense in Old Chinese, it appears to encode the directed motion sense in some cases in Middle and Modern Chinese period, as it can be followed immediately by reference objects which indicate the goal direction of the motion, as seen in (139).

(139) a. 不　敢　飞　空　往　　如来　所。(《祖堂集》)
　　　　bù　gǎn fēi kōng wǎng Rúlái　suǒ
　　　　NEG dare fly sky　go.to　Buddha place
　　　　"(He) dare not fly to sky and go to the place of Buddha."

　　　b. 或　　　有　飞　空　罗汉。(《敦煌变文》)
　　　　huò　　yǒu fēi kōng luóhàn
　　　　sometimes have fly　sky　arhat
　　　　"Sometimes there are arhats flying to the sky."

　　　c. 这　个 航班　　每天　　飞 北京。
　　　　zhè gè hángbān měitiān　fēi Běijīng
　　　　this CL flight　　every day fly Beijing
　　　　"This flight flies to Beijing every day."

　　　d. 我　明天　　飞　上海。
　　　　wǒ míngtiān fēi Shànghǎi
　　　　I　tomorrow　fly　Shanghai
　　　　"I will fly to Shanghai tomorrow."

As to these cases, I argue that contrary to the use of 飞 fēi "fly" in Old Chinese, these motion events indeed have specific contextual information promoting the inferred goal direction. It is interesting to note that in Middle and Modern Chinese the cases where 飞 fēi "fly" encodes the directed motion sense are only found to describe motion events with specific features. In Middle Chinese, the cases are in particular attested in Buddhist texts and always related to arhats or divinities flying to the sky or to the place of Buddha, which can be understood as intentional motions carried out by personalized agent with a definite goal to arrive at. In Modern Chinese, the motion events refer to the flying of airliners to their planned destinations. In other words, these goal-bound motion events provide necessary contextual information to construct the following ground objects as the goal of the motion. That is why 飞 fēi "fly" can be followed directly by goal objects in some restricted cases in Middle and Modern Chinese on the one hand, and it cannot be used in this way in Old Chinese on the other hand. However, as the verb is only found to be used in this way in a few cases and the contexts are very restrictive, the goal direction sense cannot be regarded as its lexicalized meaning; rather it is only a pragmatic sense based on the supporting contexts.

In comparison with the lexicalization patterns of 走 zǒu "run/walk", the evolution process of 飞 fēi "fly" is also represented in Figure 3. As the manner sense of 飞 fēi "fly" does not change from Old to Modern Chinese, the whole dotted square only represents its diachronic evolution of the directed motion sense. The plain arrow represents the actual lexicalization of the sense, and in contrast, the dotted arrow represents the derived pragmatic sense of the verb. The arrow with a backslash stands for the blocking of the lexicalization of certain sense. The arrows with a dotted tail illustrate the factors affecting the lexicalization or blocking of the lexicalization of the sense.

As can be seen from Figure 3, the same as 走 zǒu "run/walk", as a basic motion verb, 飞 fēi "fly" also tends to imply displacement of the theme. However, the nature of the manner encoded in 飞 fēi "fly" in Old Chinese lacks the sense of agentivity or goal-bound intention, so while 走 zǒu "run/walk" and other manner verbs such as 趋 qū "hurry up" or 奔 bēn "rush" used in the same synchronic period can lexicalize the goal direction, 飞 fēi "fly" cannot. Though 飞 fēi "fly" can get the goal direction inference in Middle and Modern Chinese, the goal direction cannot be regarded as lexicalized verbal meaning, as it is only found in restricted contexts. With a similar motivating factor as 走 zǒu "run/walk", 飞 fēi "fly" also develops a source-oriented direction in Modern Chinese.

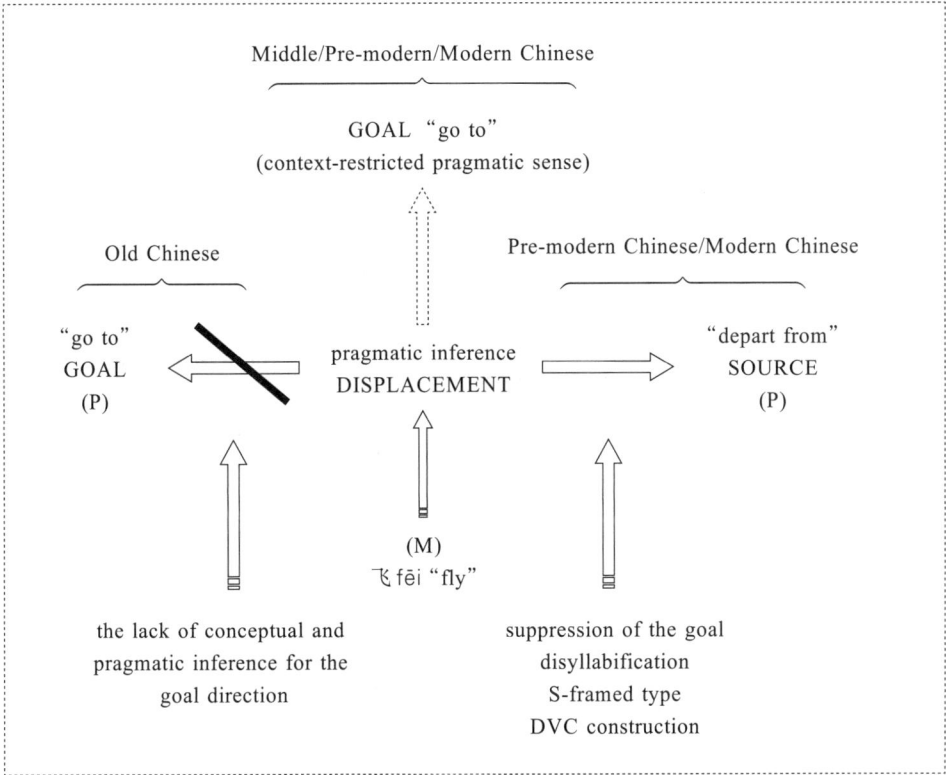

Figure 3   The Factors Affecting the Lexical Evolution of 飞 fēi "fly"

However, different from the lexicalization patterns of 飞 fēi "fly", the absence of the goal direction in 跑 pǎo "run" is due to the lack of proper morphosyntactic structures in Pre-modern Chinese. The following Figure 4 represents the evolution process of the lexicalization patterns of 跑 pǎo "run". Varied arrows used in this figure stand for the same meaning as those in Figure 3.

In Pre-modern Chinese period, the sense of the goal direction cannot be derived from manner verbs by tone alternation, as since Middle Chinese period the phonological system of Chinese has been greatly simplified, and in particular, the morphological derivation process of creating new words by changing the phonetic properties of the base words has been declined, and there is no proper morphosyntactic device that can be used to mark the derivation from the manner to the path sense. In addition, from Pre-modern Chinese the dominant syntactic devices to encode the goal path are directional complements, which are generally derived from path verbs. Without overtly expressed directional complements, manner verbs are not allowed to encode the goal direction of motion any more. Therefore, though 跑 pǎo "run" has inherited the manner sense of 走 zǒu "run/walk" in Old Chinese, it cannot lexicalize the goal path in Pre-modern Chinese.

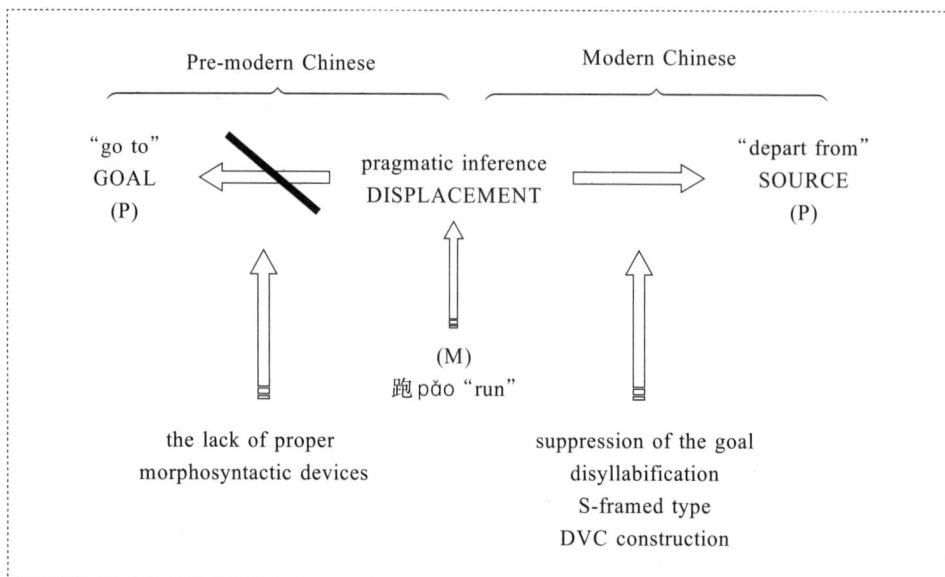

Figure 4 The Factors Affecting the Lexical Evolution of 跑 pǎo "run"

5.2.3 The Lexical Evolution of Polysemous Motion Verbs as an Epitome of the Evolution of Chinese Motion Lexicon

Though the polysemous motion verbs 走 zǒu "run/walk", 跑 pǎo "run" and 飞 fēi "fly" have distinct lexicalization patterns from other motion verbs, their lexical evolution processes from Old to Modern Chinese well reflect the general evolution trend of Chinese motion lexicon. The factors affecting their evolution processes can also account for the lexical evolution of other motion verbs. Though no other Chinese motion verbs have exactly the same lexicalization patterns or undergo similar evolution processes as the three verbs throughout the history of Chinese language, in each period of time there are verbs which pattern with these polysemous motion verbs in their lexicalization patterns.

For instance, in Old Chinese period, when the verb 走 zǒu "run" may lexicalize both the manner and goal direction of motion, its two-way ontological categorization is echoed by verbs which involve manners that are also likely to derive a pragmatic inference of displacement, such as 趋 qū "hurry up" and 奔 bēn "rush". These verbs are also polysemous, and their polysemous nature can be explained by factors that count for the lexicalization patterns of 走 zǒu "run". Similar to 走 zǒu "run", 趋 qū "hurry up" and 奔 bēn "rush" are also basic manner-of-motion verbs with high frequency of occurrence in Old Chinese. They typically describe motions featuring relatively high speed, carried out by human beings with an intention to reach a goal. Thus besides their primary manner sense, owing to their preferred pragmatic inference and favorable morphosyntactic devices (e. g. derivation through tone alternation) they also develop an independent goal-oriented path sense, which is also marked by their altered tone as the verb 走 zǒu "run".

In addition, the lexicalized goal direction in 走 zǒu "run" is also a reflection of the prominence of goal-oriented path lexicon in Old Chinese period. As discussed in Section 5.2.1, goal-oriented path verbs count the most part of path lexicon in Old Chinese. The Old Chinese path verbs listed in (140) all indicate the endpoint of the path.

(140) 到 dào "arrive"   至 zhì "arrive"   造 zào "arrive"
　　　 诣 yì "go.to"   就 jiù "come.near.to"   即 jí "come.near.to"
　　　 如 rú "go.to"   适 shì "go.to"   逝 shì "arrive"
　　　 踵 zhǒng "go.to"   之 zhī "arrive"   及 jí "go.to"
　　　 赴 fù "go.to"

The lexicalization patterns of these goal-oriented path verbs are consistent with the lexicalized goal direction sense in 走 zǒu "run" and both reflect the language's typological property as a verb-framed language, i. e. the core schema of motion events is predominantly rendered into verbs. Therefore, the effect of the interaction between conceptual meaning and morphosyntactic structures available in the language at certain synchronic period is not only verified by the lexicalization patterns of the polysemous motion verbs but also apply to the whole motion lexicon.

The similar lexical evolution processes of the polysemous motion verbs and other path verbs in the later developmental stages of Chinese language also support this point. For example, since the Middle Chinese period due to the change of the morphosyntactic structure of Chinese (e.g. phonological simplification, disyllabification, etc.) and its typological shift from verb-framed to satellite-framed language, the goal direction sense of 走 zǒu "run" has become disfavored and declines greatly. Its lexical change in this line also parallels to lexical evolution of other motion verbs. The most conspicuous one is the parallel decline of those goal-oriented path verbs in (140). Very similar to the verb 走 zǒu "run", most of these path verbs also lose their goal direction sense, though different from 走 zǒu "run" after they lose this sense they cannot be used as motion verbs altogether, because the goal path sense is the only meaning component encoded in these verbs. Based on her survey in texts composed in Middle Chinese period, Ma (2008) notes that the verbs 如 rú "go to", 逝 shì "go to", 踵 zhǒng "arrive" and 适 shì "go to" cannot be used as motion verbs in Middle Chinese period, and though some other verbs such as 造 zào "arrive" and 赴 fù "go to" can still be used as motion verbs to indicate the goal direction, their uses are very restricted only representing the relics of their Old Chinese use or as bounded morphemes forming compound verbs with another morpheme such as 造访 zào fǎng "go visit", 赴宴 fù yàn "attend banquet", etc. Thus it is evident that factors such as simplification of phonological and morphological system, the tendency of disyllabification and change of framing type of the language, which affect the evolution of the verb 走 zǒu "run" also have effect on the evolution of these path verbs.

Therefore though on the surface the lexicalization patterns of the polysemous motion verbs discussed in this chapter are different from other verbs and the factors affecting their diachronic lexical evolution seem to be unique to their distinct lexicalization patterns, the data in Chinese indicate that the fact is just the contrary: the lexical evolution of these verbs is an epitome of the lexical evolution of the entire motion lexicon. The factors related to the conceptualization of motion events, pragmatic use and typological features of the language at different synchronic periods have effect on the evolution of other motion verbs as well. The two-way interaction between the conceptual components of verbs and the morphosyntactic structure of the language is attested in lexicalization patterns of motion verbs in general.

5.3 Summary

The diachronic evolution of the three polysemous verbs results from the interaction of various factors such as pragmatic inference and cognitive preference that these verbs are associated with as well as the available morphosyntactic devices of the language in certain synchronic period. There is cognitive and pragmatic motivation for their distinct lexicalization patterns, but the morphosyntactic structures of Chinese at certain synchronic period also affect their actual lexicalization patterns. Verbal meaning and grammatical constructions have two-way interactions. Not only the lexical semantics of verbs determines what grammatical construction a verb may be used in, grammatical constructions may also affect a verb's lexical meaning.

To view the diachronic evolution of the three verbs in general, it can be found that the distinct lexicalization patterns are not accidental; rather different evolution lines are motivated by the similar mechanism, and both pragmatic inference obtained from the contexts in the process of language use and the favorable morphosyntactic structures are necessary conditions for the lexicalization of a new sense. Though the three verbs are all manner verbs and they are associated with the displacement inference pragmatically, on the one hand, whether or not they may lexicalize certain directed motion sense depends on whether there is an invited pragmatic inference of the specific direction; on the other hand, it also depends on whether there are proper morphosyntactic structures which could provide favorable devices for the lexicalization of the sense. Therefore, the distinct lexicalization patterns of the three verbs are motivated by various factors such as pragmatic inference, typological change of Chinese, the emergence or decline of certain grammatical constructions and grammaticalization of path-indicating elements in motion constructions. However, these factors affecting the lexical evolution of these polysemous motion verbs may also be extended to account for the diachronic evolution of other Chinese motion verbs, so their evolution process represents an epitome of the evolution of the entire Chinese motion lexicon.

Chapter 6

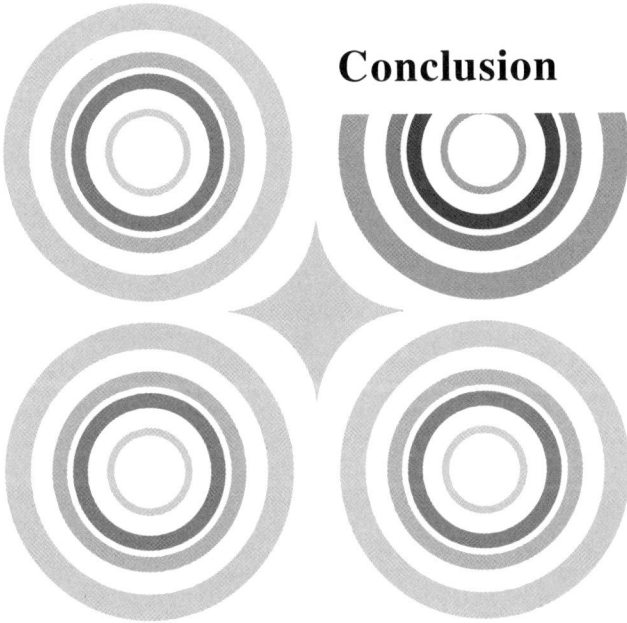

Conclusion

This chapter summarizes the major findings of the present study and discusses relevant issues related to motion events and motion verbs at the lexicon and syntax interface. The grammatical behaviors of polysemous manner-of-motion verbs in Chinese are reviewed in comparison with manner-of-motion verbs in other languages. The status of lexical semantics is discussed with reference to construction meaning. The factors affecting the diachronic change of lexicalization patterns of motion verbs are also summarized. Future work in the field is also suggested.

6.1 Summary of Major Findings of the Present Study

Assuming verbal meaning can be represented by predicate decomposition and a verb's grammatical behavior can be predicted from its lexical meaning, based on the regular correspondence between certain semantic component encoded in verbs and the syntactic structure they appear in. Verbs are argued to fall into natural semantic groups. The semantic notions of manner and result show complementary distributions in verbal meaning and have contrastive consequences with regard to verbs' grammatical behaviors. The MRC hypothesis constrains what meaning components a verbal root may lexicalize. Most potential counterexample verbs in English dissolve if a careful distinction is made between the lexical semantics and the pragmatic inference from the contexts. The linguistic phenomena corresponding to the MRC cannot be reduced to different syntactic configurations a verb is freely used in or differences in aspectual focus of verbs; rather it is a well-motivated principle operating in the lexicon.

As to the notions of manner and result in Chinese motion events, though varied conceptual properties related to manner or path verbs are proposed by scholars, not all conceptual properties are relevant to ontological categorization of motion verbs in Chinese. For example, the conceptual properties concerning the force of gravity, the medium of motion are not regarded as a separate manner sense of the verb, since they do not encode independent changes and are encyclopedic knowledge of the conceptualization of motion events in the language. A re-examination of motion verbs collected by Chen and Guo (2009) reveals that to some degree the controversies over the classification of some less prototypical motion verbs are related to misunderstood manner concepts or unclear criteria for testing manner or path meaning components. Judged from a set of tests, the controversies are solved by proposing a consistent classification of controversial verbs. The purported counterexample verbs are explained based on both notions of manner and path and checked with relevant tests. They are shown to lexicalize only one type of meaning components. Inconsistent grammatical behaviors of three motion verbs 走 zǒu "walk", 跑 pǎo "run" and 飞 fēi "fly", which are all neglected in previous studies, are in particular looked at in detail. When these verbs are used following another verb expressing a distinct manner or in a subject inversion construction, they only encode a direction of motion as "depart from a reference object" dropping the manner sense. Thus these verbs are polysemous motion verbs encoding the two senses separately conforming to the MRC hypothesis.

Though Old Chinese is a typologically distinct language from Modern Chinese, motion verbs in Old Chinese can also be categorized by their ontological type as manner or result verbs. Through the compatibility test for the motion verbs used in serial verb constructions in representative Old Chinese texts, it is shown that manner and path verbs in Old Chinese show different compatibilities with other verbs expressing manner or path information. In a single integral motion event, whereas Old Chinese manner verbs are compatible with verbs expressing varied path information, path verbs can co-occur with verbs indicating a wide range of manner information. Detailed analysis of counterexample verbs to the MRC in Old Chinese proposed by researchers (Ma, 2008; Shi, Wu, 2014, 2015) demonstrates that these verbs encode only one type of meaning at a time. To be specific, these counterexample verbs either are polysemous verbs encoding the two meaning components separately or lexicalize only one meaning component deriving the other from the contexts. Old Chinese verbs like 走 zǒu "run", 趋 qū "hurry up" and 奔 bēn "rush" belong to the former type. These verbs in their basic uses are manner verbs, but when they are following by locative nouns which indicate the goal of motion they always undergo ontological shift from manner to path verbs through tone alternation. Verbs like 逃 táo "flee", 亡 wáng "flee", 遁 dùn "flee", 涉 shè "sail across" and 渡 dù "sail across" belong to the latter type. 逃 táo "flee", 亡 wáng "flee" and 遁 dùn "flee" are in fact manner verbs deriving the direction of motion from the contexts. 渡 dù "sail across" and 涉 shè "sail across" are path verbs with more elaborated path information. Their lexicalization patterns reflect the typological properties of verb-framed languages, which tend to have larger path lexicon including path verbs with both relatively abstract and more elaborated path information.

In Modern Chinese, manner-of-motion verbs 走 zǒu "walk", 跑 pǎo "run" and 飞 fēi "fly" are different from other manner verbs because they are polysemous and exhibit dual ways of ontological categorization. The diachronic investigation of the evolution of their lexical meaning and grammatical behaviors shows that a verb's ontological category as the manner or result and their relevant grammatical behaviors are not only determined by the concepts they are associated with but also affected by available morphosyntactic structures of the language. The verb 走 zǒu "run/ walk" may encode both the manner and direction of motion in both Old and Modern Chinese, but along with the language's evolution from Old to Modern Chinese its lexical meaning and grammatical behaviors have also changed. In Old Chinese besides being used as a manner verb, it may also be directly followed by locative nouns encoding the goal-oriented direction of motion, but in Modern Chinese it cannot be used in this way any more and correspondingly its lexicalized direction has changed into the source-oriented path. The possible factors affecting its evolution are analyzed. The pragmatic inference of displacement associated with nature of manner encoded in these verbs and the cognitive preference for the goal-oriented path in the conceptualization of motion events provide conceptual basis for the lexicalization of the directed motion sense in the verb. In addition, available morphosyntactic structures in specific developmental stages of the Chinese language facilitate or prohibit the actual lexicalization of either the goal- or source-oriented path sense. In Old Chinese, more complicated phonological and morphological system provides beneficiary morphosyntactic devices for the verb to derive a new sense without changing its written form. The verb-framed language property that prototypically renders the goal-oriented path into verbs also promotes the lexicalization of the goal direction in the manner verb. In contrast, from Middle to Modern Chinese period, gradually simplified phonological system, disyllabification tendency of Chinese and its typological shift from verb-framed to satellite-framed language make the encoding of the goal direction in verbs unfavorable on the one hand. On the other hand the interaction between the inferred displacement from the manner verb and the newly emerged directional verbal compound construction consolidates the source-oriented sense to be lexicalized. Though the verb 跑 pǎo "run" and 飞 fēi "fly" have undergone different evolution processes from Old to Modern Chinese, their distinct lexicalization patterns can also be explained by the relevant factors affecting the evolution process of 走 zǒu "run/walk". The natures of manner encoded in the three verbs are all likely to obtain a displacement inference, but in Old Chinese distinct from the verb 走 zǒu "run" which is prototypically used to encode motion events carried out by human beings often with an obvious intention of reaching a goal, 飞 fēi "fly" is only used to encode motion events related to animals which cannot possibly have an intention of reaching a goal. Thus, without a favorable pragmatic concept associated with a goal direction, even with proper morphosyntactic devices 飞 fēi "fly" does not develop a lexicalized goal direction in Old Chinese. Though the verb 跑 pǎo "run" encodes the similar manner of motion as 走 zǒu "run", it enters Chinese lexicon much later, i.e. in Pre-modern Chinese period, when along with the typological change of Chinese there is no favorable morphosyntactic resources for the verb to develop the goal direction, so it does not have a separate goal-oriented path sense throughout its evolution process. However, the same as 走 zǒu "walk", since Pre-modern Chinese period both 飞 fēi "fly" and 跑 pǎo "run" have benefited from the interaction between their inferred displacement concept related to the nature of manner they encode and the property of the directional verbal compound construction, their source-oriented direction sense has been developed and consolidated. The evolution of the lexicalization patterns of the three verbs demonstrates that the notions of manner and result reveal the two-way interaction between the lexicon and the syntactic structures.

6.2 Motion Verbs and Motion Constructions at the Lexicon and Syntax Interface

6.2.1 Polysemous Manner-of-Motion Verbs in Cross-Linguistic Contexts

As shown by the diachronic and synchronic evidence, the three Chinese manner-of-motion verbs have two separate lexicalized senses as manner or path verbs in certain developmental period of the Chinese language. This fact is distinct from the observation made by Levin et al. (2009) in other languages, as they argue that cross-linguistically manner-of-motion verbs share the same type of verb roots: they all specify only the manner of motion and the sense of the directed motion arises from pragmatic factors. In their study, Levin et al. examine the manner-of-motion verbs across Germanic and Romance languages and illustrate that pragmatic factors such as the nature of manner the verb specifies, the aspectual feature of the motion events and the property of ground object all have effect on the direction motion reading of manner verbs. For example, verbs describing simpler, punctual motion in a less elaborated path to a locative place with clear boundaries are more likely to have a direction motion reading. In other words, manner-of-motion verbs across Germanic and Romance languages are not polysemous and they may be categorized as only one ontological type. One of the few verbs Levin and Rappaport Hovav (2013) do mention that have the directed motion sense is *climb* in English. However, according to them, in its basic uses climb only encodes the manner of motion but when used to describe the motion of abstract categories such as price, temperature, etc., it encodes an upward directed motion sense but not manner, as seen in (141). Because the directed motion sense of climb is only restricted to abstract categories, the lexicalization of the sense may be due to the abstraction and metaphorical use of the verbal meaning.

(141) The price/temperature climbs.

Nevertheless in the case of the three verbs in Chinese, their directed motion sense is used across different contexts within or beyond the concrete motion events by various themes, whether animate or not. Moreover, besides the three verbs, there are other manner-of-motion verbs which also show two-way lexicalization patterns. For example, in Old Chinese, besides 走 zǒu "run/walk", other manner-of-motion verbs such as 奔 bēn "rush", 趋 qū "hurry up", and 超 chāo "surpass" also show similar lexicalization patterns to be categorized as either manner or path verbs. This indicates the two-way categorization of the three Chinese motion verbs in question should not be regarded as coincidences or metaphorical use of these verbs. Then why do these manner-of-motion verbs in Chinese show distinct lexicalization patterns from manner-of-motion verbs in other languages? Probably the properties of the morphosyntactic structure and the evolution of motion event framing can provide some hints to the question. On the one hand, different from other satellite-framed languages such as Russian, Chinese is a typical isolating language which has limited functional categories to express the abstract spatial relation in motion events. In Chinese most elements describing spatial relation including prepositions and directional complements are evolved from verbs (Xu, 2013). On the other hand, Chinese also allows serial verb constructions in which more than one verb can be used in sequence without morphological marking to indicate subordination or coordination. These morphosyntactic properties of Chinese language provide manner verbs favorable grammatical environment to undergo the process of categorical change. In addition, along the evolution from verb-framed to satellite-framed language most path elements are derived from verbs, in particular path verbs. It can be attested from the fact that most directional complements such as 来 lái "come", 去 qù "go", 上 shàng "ascend", 下 xià "descend", 回 huí "return" and 进 jìn "enter" in Modern Chinese can still be used as the main verb in sentences. The grammaticalization from path verbs to satellites provides favorable morphosyntactic contexts for manner-of-motion verbs to derive the directed motion sense through analogy. Thus manner-of-motion verbs with favorable pragmatic inference such as 走 zǒu "walk", 跑 pǎo "run" and 飞 fēi "fly" also develop a separate path sense and have been further grammaticalized as directional complements.

6.2.2 Lexical Semantics and Morphosyntactic Structure

How to explain the varied grammatical behaviors of a verb is one of the key issues at the interface between lexicon and syntactic structures. The lexical semantic approach takes the position that grammatical behaviors of verbs are determined by the lexical semantics, and in particular, the ontological type of verbs. As most verbs have only one ontological type, if a verb exhibits varied grammatical behaviors which correspond to two different ontological types, the less prototypical use of the verb may be attributed to the pragmatic inference from the contexts. Under this assumption, since a verbal root has a basic association with a certain event structure position, the polysemous verbs should not be very widespread and it is possible to identify certain pragmatic factors which promote the inferred meaning and supporting contexts in which the derived lexical sense is used (Rappaport Hovav, Levin, 2010). In addition, based on the distinction between structural and idiosyncratic meaning components in verbs, advocates of the lexical semantic approach also assume the idiosyncratic meaning is not grammatically relevant, which only differentiates the members within an ontological type. In their in-depth studies of verbs like clean, cut and climb, Rappaport Hovav and Levin argue these verbs are basically associated with only one ontological type, and under certain circumstances they undergo a categorical shift to other types. For example, the verb cut is basically a result verb, but when used in conative constructions it changes into a manner verb dropping the result sense. However, for polysemous Chinese motion verbs, neither the manner nor the path sense is strictly restricted to certain pragmatic factors or contexts. As argued in Chapter 2 without supporting pragmatic factors manner-of-motion verbs such as 走 zǒu "walk" can also have the directed motion sense. What more, in Old Chinese polysemous motion verbs are not restricted to the three verbs; rather there are a group of manner verbs such as 奔

bēn "rush", 趋 qū "hurry up", and 超 chāo "surpass", which also show similar lexicalization patterns. These facts indicate pragmatic factors related to lexical semantics of verbs alone cannot completely explain the whole picture.

The construction approach to argument structure (Goldberg, 1995, 2006) is also designated to explain verbs with varied grammatical behaviors. According to this approach, verbs with varied grammatical behaviors are mainly determined by construction meaning, and it is not necessary to posit different lexical entries for the same verb. Rather verbs are monosemous: their meaning is the "core" meaning that persists across all their uses. However, verbs and syntactic structures have two-way interactions. On the one hand, semantic evolution of these Chinese motion verbs show that if the conceptual components of verbs are compatible with specific constructions in certain synchronic period, the verbs can be used in the construction, which promotes certain pragmatic inference to be derived from the primary meaning of the verb. On the other hand, lexicon and syntax form a continuum and the relationship between verbs and constructions is interdependent in that the verb itself is liable to change through repetitive use in constructions, which may ultimately result in the lexicalization of a new sense of the verb. Therefore, ontological categorization of verbs and their grammatical behaviors could not be attributed to either conceptual components or construction meaning alone; rather they result from the dynamic interaction of lexical semantics and syntactic constructions.

6.2.3 Diachronic Change of the Lexicalization Patterns of Motion Verbs

The diachronic change of the lexicalization patterns of motion verbs is regulated by general lexical principles operating in semantic structure of verbs on the one hand, and on the other hand, it is also affected by other factors such as the conventional pragmatic inference from the contexts and morphosyntactic resources of the language at certain developmental stage. From a diachronic perspective, the evolution of the lexical semantics of manner-of-motion verbs in Chinese proves the existence of a separate semantic structure at the lexicon and syntax interface which is reflected through lexical principles which constrain what information can be packed in a verb. The notions of manner and result are two linguistically relevant semantic categories which reflect the organization of semantic structures in verbal meaning. Along with the evolutionary process of Chinese language, motion verbs with variable grammatical behaviors may change their specific lexical semantics and may be used in different syntactic structures, but the packed information in their lexical semantics is always constrained by the semantic structure represented as the MRC principle. For example, from Old to Modern Chinese the three verbs studied in the present study 走 zǒu "run/walk", 跑 pǎo "run" and 飞 fēi "fly" have changed their specific semantics and the syntactic structures they may appear in have also altered, but in each stage of the development they never lexicalize the two meaning components manner and result together. This is the direct evidence for the existence of the lexical constraint operating in semantic representations of verbs. However, besides the lexical principle constraining the general lexicalization patterns of meaning components, the specific manner or result encoded in these verbs may be affected by other factors. For instance, the verb 飞 fēi "fly" is polysemous encoding the manner and direction of motion in its different uses in Modern Chinese, but it is not polysemous in Old Chinese due to a lack of proper pragmatic inference of the goal of direction from the nature of manner it encodes. In addition, the diachronic evolution of lexicalization patterns of motion verbs is affected by available morphosyntactic resources of the language. In Pre-modern Chinese the verb 跑 pǎo "run" encodes a similar manner component as the verb 走 zǒu "run" in Old Chinese, but it cannot encode the goal direction of motion as the verb 走 zǒu "run" does because there are not favorable morphosyntactic structures for the goal direction encoding in verbs in Pre-modern Chinese period. Though synchronically the grammatical behavior of a motion verb conforms to its ontological categorization, its diachronic evolution in ontological type and specific lexical semantics may be affected by a variety of factors.

6.3 Future Work

The scope of the present study is mainly based on the lexicalization patterns of

Chinese motion verbs and constructions. However, the MRC hypothesis is also demonstrated validly in the change of state domain. Whether the Chinese verbs in the change of state domain also conform to the MRC hypothesis needs further study. Researchers (Tai, 1984; Xiao, McEnery, 2004) argue that there are no mono-morphemic accomplishment verbs in Chinese. Change of state events are mainly expressed by resultative verbal compounds, which are composed of two verbs with the first one expressing the action and the second indicating the state an entity achieves as a result of the action. For example, in (142), in the resultative verb compound 打碎 dǎsuì "hit break" the verb 打 dǎ "hit" expresses an action of hitting and the verb 碎 suì "break" indicates the state the vase achieves.

(142) 他 打 碎　了　一　只　花瓶。
　　　tā dǎ suì　le　yì　zhī huāpíng
　　　he hit break ASP one CL　flower bottle
　　　"He broke a vase."

Thus it can be seen that the manner and result of a complex event are represented with two verbal roots conforming to the MRC hypothesis.

However, the syntactic distributions of some verbs indicate that things may not be as straightforward as they appear to be. In RVCs, some verbs may be used as both the first verb and the second verb. For example, in (143), the verb 哭 kū "cry" is used as the first verb in the RVC 哭红 kū hóng "cry red" to express the action of the event and thus it does not convey the information of result, but in (144) the verb 哭 kū "cry" used as the second verb in the RVC 吓哭 xià kū "scare cry" seems to indicate a state the baby achieves.

(143) 她 哭 红　了　　眼睛。
　　　tā kū　hóng le　　yǎnjīng
　　　she cry red　ASP eye
　　　"Her eyes became red as a result of her crying."

(144) 陌生人　　　　吓　哭了　　宝宝。

　　　mòshēngrén xià kū le　bǎobǎo

　　　stranger　　　scare cry ASP　baby

　　　"The stranger scared the baby into crying."

Then the questions are as an action verb why the verb 哭 kū "cry" also expresses the resultative state an entity achieves and whether it conveys two types of meaning components manner and result. It deserves further investigation.

Moreover, compared with motion events, change of state events are more complicated. The ontological status of other verbs also needs further investigation. For example, as argued by researchers that the semantics of the verb 杀 shā "kill" in Chinese is different from its counterpart in English, as it does not necessarily entail a caused result state of death. It can be seen from the contrastive readings of the pair of sentences in (145).

(145) a. *John killed Mary, but Mary did not die.

　　　b. 约翰　　杀　了　　玛丽，可是　玛丽 没　死。

　　　　 Yuēhàn shā le　　Mǎli　kěshì Mǎli méi sǐ

　　　　 John　kill ASP Mary　but　Mary NEG die

　　　　 "#John killed Mary, but Mary did not die."

Though in the English sentence (145)a the death of the patient Mary cannot be cancelled, the patient in the Chinese sentence (145)b may survive the event expressed by the verb 杀 shā "kill". Thus though the English verb kill is a definitely result verb, the ontological status of the Chinese verb 杀 shā "kill" is not so easy to determine. On the one hand, it does not necessarily entail a caused result, so it cannot be regarded as a result verb. On the other hand, 杀 shā "kill" does not encode any specific way of action either, as it may denote any action with an intention of causing the patient to die. Thus the ontological status of change of state verbs like 杀 shā "kill" in Chinese still needs further investigation so as to check the validity of the MRC hypothesis.

Finally, the diachronic evolution of change of state verbs is also a topic for future study. As demonstrated in previous chapters, though motion verbs in both Old and Modern Chinese conform to the hypothesis, along with the evolution of Chinese language, affected by a variety of factors (e.g. pragmatic, cognitive, morphosyntactic factors, etc.), the ontological categorization and grammatical behaviors of motion verbs have changed. As is observed by researchers (Sun, 2013), the grammatical behaviors of change of state verbs in Old Chinese is also different from Modern Chinese. For example, though it is generally accepted there are no monomorphemic accomplishment verbs in Modern Chinese, there are verbs of this kind in Old Chinese. For example, as can be seen in (146), the monomorphemic verb 破 pò "destroy" unlike its counterpart in Modern Chinese can be used to express an accomplishment event.

(146) 击　　李　由　军　　破　　　　之。(《史记》)
　　　 jī　　Lǐ　Yóu　jūn　　pò　　　　zhī
　　　 attack Li You　army　**destroy　it**
　　　 "He attacked Li You's army and destroyed it."

Similarly, though the verb 杀 shā "kill" in Modern Chinese does not entail a resultative state death, in Old Chinese it does entail the death of the patient. The questions are: whether change of state verbs in Old Chinese adhere to the MRC hypothesis, whether change of state verbs have also undergone similar evolutionary process and whether the identified factors which affect the evolution process of motion verbs also apply to change of state verbs. These questions all deserve further investigation. Studies on these questions will shed light on a more accurate and comprehensive understanding of lexicalization patterns of Chinese verbs and the validity of the lexical principle.

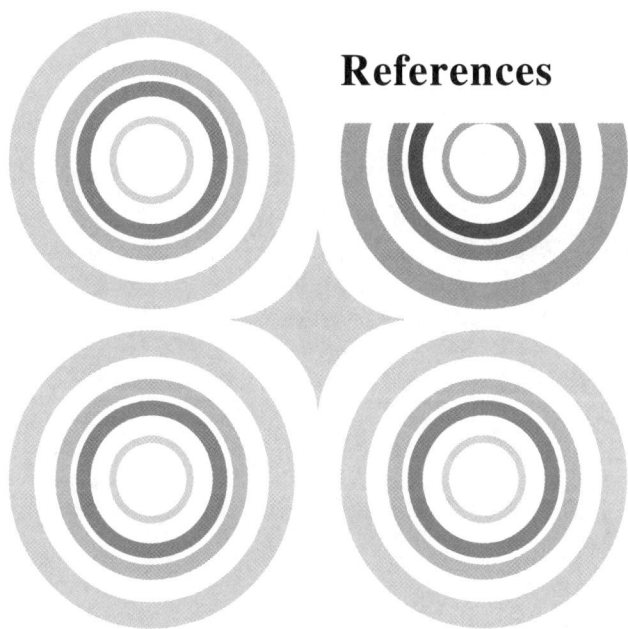

References

ACEDO-MATELLÁN V, MATEU J, 2010. From syntax to roots: a syntactic approach to root ontologies[R]. Stuttgart: University of Stuttgart.

ALDRIDGE L E, 2012. What's in a verb? Evidence from manner/result complementarity [D]. London: University College London.

ALLEN S, OZYÜREK A, KITA S, et al., 2007. Language specific and universal influences in children's syntactic packaging of manner and path: a comparison of English, Japanese, and Turkish[J]. Cognition, 102: 16-48.

BAI Y, 2007. Diachronic and synchronic comparative study of the meaning system of "walk"[J]. Journal of Shanxi University, 30(2): 81-85.

BAXTER W H, 1992. A handbook of old Chinese phonology[M]. Berlin: De Gruyter Mouton.

BAXTER W H, SAGART L, 1998. Word formation in old Chinese[M]//PACKARD J L. New approaches to Chinese word formation: morphology, phonology, and the lexicon in modern and ancient Chinese. Berlin: De Gruyter Mouton.

BEAVERS J, KOONTZ-GARBODEN A, 2012. Manner and result in the roots of verbal meaning[J]. Linguistic inquiry, 43(3): 331-369.

BEAVERS J, LEVIN B, THAM S W, 2010. A morphosyntactic basis for variation in the encoding of motion events[J]. Journal of linguistics, 46: 331-377.

BIALY A, 2013. On manner/result complementarity[J]. Studies in Polish linguistics, 8(4): 151-171.

BOUCHARD D, 1995. The semantics of syntax: a minimalist approach to grammar [M]. Chicago, IL: University of Chicago Press.

CHAO Y R, 1968. A grammar of spoken Chinese[M]. Berkeley: University of California Press.

CHEN L, GUO J S, 2009. Motion events in Chinese novels: evidence for an equipollently-framed language[J]. Journal of pragmatics, 41: 1749-1766.

DOWNER G B, 1959. Derivation by tone-change in classical Chinese[J]. Bulletin of the school of oriental and African studies, 22(2): 258-290.

ERTESCHIK-SHIR N, RAPOPORT T, 2010. Contact and other results[M]// RAPPAPORT HOVAV M, DORON E, SICHEL I. Lexical semantics, syntax, and event structure. Oxford: Oxford University Press.

FAN S Y, 2013. Argument structure in mandarin Chinese: a lexical-syntactic perspective[D]. Madrid: Autonomous University of Madrid.

FILLMORE C J, 1997. Lectures on deixis[M]. Stanford, CA: CSLI Publications.

FLEISCHHAUER J, GAMERSCHLAG T, 2014. We're going through changes: how change of state verbs and arguments combine in scale composition[J]. Lingua, 141: 30-47.

FOLLI R, RAMCHAND G, 2005. Prepositions and results in Italian and English: an analysis from event decomposition[M]//VERKUYL H, DE SWART H, VAN HOUT A. Perspectives on aspect. Dordrecht: Kluwer Academic Publishers.

GOLDBERG A E, 1995. Constructions: a construction grammar approach to argument structure[M]. Chicago, IL: University of Chicago Press.

GOLDBERG A E, 2006. Constructions at work: the nature of generalization in language[M]. Oxford: Oxford University Press.

GOLDBERG A E, 2010. Verbs, constructions, and semantic frames[M]//DORON E, RAPPAPORT HOVAV M, SICHEL I. Syntax lexical semantics, and event structure. Oxford: Oxford University Press.

GOLDBERG A E, JACKENDOFF R, 2004. The English resultative as a family of constructions[J]. Language, 80(3): 532-568.

GUO X L, 1986. Handbook of historical pronunciation of Chinese characters[M]. Beijing: Peking University Press.

HARLEY H, 2005. How do verbs get their names? Denominal verbs, manner incorporation and the ontology of verb roots in English[M]//ERTESCHIK-SHIR N, RAPOPORT T. The syntax of aspect. Oxford: Oxford University Press.

HOEKSTRA T, MULDER R, 1990. Unergatives as copular verbs: locational and existential predication[J]. The linguistic review, 7(1): 1-80.

HSIAO H, 2009. Motion event descriptions and manner-of-motion verbs in mandarin [D]. Buffalo: The State University of New York at Buffalo.

HUSBAND E M, 2011. Rescuing manner/result complementarity from certain death [C]. Proceedings of the 47th Annual Chicago Linguistics Society.

IHARA H, FUJITA I, 2000. A cognitive approach to errors in case marking in Japanese agrammatism: the priority of the goal-ni over the source-kara[M]// FOOLEN A, VAN DER LEEK F. Constructions in cognitive linguistics: selected papers from the fifth international cognitive linguistics conference. Amsterdam: John Benjamins Publishing Company.

IKEGAMI Y, 1987. "Source" vs. "goal": a case of linguistic dissymmetry[M]// DIRVEN R, RADDEN G. Concepts of case. Tübingen: Narr.

JACKENDOFF R, 1983. Semantics and cognition[M]. Cambridge, MA: MIT Press.

JACKENDOFF R, 1987. The status of thematic relations in linguistic theory[J]. Linguistic inquiry, 18: 369-411.

JACKENDOFF R, 1990. Semantic structures[M]. Cambridge, MA: MIT Press.

JACKENDOFF R, 1997. The architecture of the language faculty[M]. Cambridge, MA: MIT Press.

JACKENDOFF R, 2002. Foundations of language: brain, meaning, grammar, evolution[M]. Oxford: Oxford University Press.

JIANG J C, WU F X, 1997. A compendium of pre-modern Chinese[M]. Changsha: Hunan Education Press.

KABATA K, 2013. Goal-source asymmetry and cross-linguistic grammaticalization patterns: a cognitive-typological approach[J]. Language sciences, 36: 78-89.

KALLGREN G, 1958. Studies in Sung time colloquial Chinese as revealed in Chu Hi's Ts'uanshu[J]. Bulletin of the museum of far eastern antiquities, 30: 1-65.

KENNEDY C, 2001. Polar opposition and the ontology of "degrees"[J]. Linguistics and philosophy, 24: 33-70.

KENNEDY C, MCNALLY L, 2005. Scale structure and the semantic typology of gradable predicates[J]. Language, 81(2): 345-381.

KIPARSKY P, 1997. Remarks on denominal verbs[M]//ALSINA A, BRESNAN J,

汉语位移动词中的方式结果互补性研究——共时与历时视角

| | | | | | | | | | | | The Manner/Result Complementarity in Chinese Motion Verbs: Synchronic and Diachronic Perspectives

SELLS P. Complex predicates. Stanford: CSLI Publications.

KITAHARA H, 2009. The parallelism between motion constructions and resultative constructions based on the lexical conceptual structure and the scale structure and syntactic structure of "Ni" phrases[M]. Tokyo: Hituzi-Syobo.

KUBOTA Y, 2014. Aspectual composition with motion verbs in Japanese: a scale-based account[EB/OL]. (2017-05-05) [2019-07-10]. http://www. u. tsukuba. ac. jp/~kubota.yusuke. fn/papers/papers. html#ms.

LAKUSTA M L, LANDAU B, 2005. Starting at the end: the importance of goals in spatial language[J]. Cognition, 96: 1-33.

LAKUSTA M L, LANDAU B, 2012. Language and memory for motion events: origins of the asymmetry between goal and source paths[J]. Cognitive science, 36 (3): 517-544.

LAMARRE C, 2008. The linguistic categorization of deictic direction in Chinese: with reference to Japanese[M]//XU D. Space in languages of China: cross-linguistic, synchronic and diachronic perspectives. Dordrecht: Springer.

LAMARRE C, 2013. The evolution of directional verbal compound V-zou and its motivation[M]//HIDEKI K. Studies on Chinese grammar in honor of professor Kimura Hideki. Tokyo: Hakuteisha.

LEVIN B, RAPPAPORT H M, 1991. Wiping the slate clean: a lexical semantic exploration[J]. Cognition, 41: 123-151.

LEVIN B, RAPPAPORT H M, 1995. Unaccusativity: at the syntax-lexical semantics interface[M]. Cambridge, MA: MIT Press.

LEVIN B, RAPPAPORT H M, 2005. Argument realization[M]. Cambridge: Cambridge University Press.

LEVIN B, BEAVERS J, THAMS W, 2009. Manner of motion roots across languages: same or different? [M]. Stuttgart: University of Stuttgart.

LEVIN B, RAPPAPORT H M, 2011. Lexical conceptual structure[M]//HEUSINGER K, MAIENBORN C, PORTNER P. Semantics: an international handbook of natural language meaning. Berlin: De Gruyter Mouton.

LEVIN B, RAPPAPORT H M, 2013. Lexicalized meaning and manner/result complementarity[M]//ARSENIJEVIĆ B, GEHRKE B, MARÍN R. Studies in the composition and decomposition of event predicates. Dordrecht: Springer.

LEVIN B, RAPPAPORT H M, 2014. Lexicalization patterns[M]//TRUSWELL R. Oxford handbook of event structure. Oxford: Oxford University Press.

LI C N, THOMPSON S A, 1981. Mandarin Chinese: a functional reference grammar [M]. Berkeley: University of California Press.

LI S C, 2007. Analysis of middle Chinese morphology based on disyllable data[J]. Journal of Ningxia University, 29(3): 1-8.

LI Y-H A, 1990. Order and constituency in mandarin Chinese[M]. Dordrecht: Kluwer Academic.

LIN J X, 2011. The encoding of motion events in Chinese: multi-morpheme motion constructions [D]. Stanford: Stanford University.

LIN J X, PECK J, 2011. The syntax-semantics interface of multi-morpheme motion constructions in Chinese: an analysis based on hierarchical scalar structure[J]. Studies in language, 35(2): 337-379.

LIU Y H, 1998. On directional complements[M]. Beijing: Beijing Language and Culture University Press.

LYU S X, 1963. A preliminary study of the problem of monosyllabism and disyllabism in modern Chinese[J]. Studies of the Chinese language (1): 11-23.

MA Y X, 2008. The development of chinese path verbs and motion event expressions[M]. Beijing: China Minzu University Press.

MALT B C, GENNARI S, IMAI M, et al., 2008. Talking about walking: biomechanics and the change of locomotion[J]. Psychological science, 19: 232-240.

MATEU J, ACEDO-MATELL'AN V, 2012. The manner/result complementarity revisited: a syntactic approach[M]//CUERVO M C, ROBERGE Y. The end of argument structure. Bingley: Emerald.

NAMIKI S, 2012. A pragmatic account of co-occurrence of manner-of-motion verbs with ni-phrases interpreted as goal in Japanese[J]. Tsukuba English studies, 31: 85-102.

NARASIMHAN B, 1998. The encoding of complex events in Hindi and English [D]. Boston: Boston University.

■ 汉语位移动词中的方式结果互补性研究——共时与历时视角

| | | | | | | | | | | | | The Manner/Result Complementarity in Chinese Motion Verbs: Synchronic and Diachronic Perspectives

NEELEMAN A, VAN DE KOOT H, 2010. The linguistic expression of causation [R]. Working Papers in Linguistics University College London.

NIKITINA T, 2008. Pragmatic factors and variation in the expression of spatial goals: the case of into vs. in[M]//ASBURY A, GEHRKE B, NOUWEN R, et al., Syntax and semantics of spatial P. Amsterdam: John Benjamins Publishing Company.

NORMAN J, 1988. Chinese[M]. Cambridge: Cambridge University Press.

ONO N, 2010. A lexical resource view of motion and resultative constructions[R]. Paper Presented at MLF 2010, National Institute for Japanese Language and Linguistics, Tokyo.

PACKARD J L, 1998. A lexical phonology of Mandarin Chinese[M]//PACKARD J L. New approaches to Chinese word formation: morphology, phonology, and the lexicon in modern and ancient Chinese. Berlin: De Gruyter Mouton.

PACKARD J L, 2000. The morphology of Chinese[M]. Cambridge: Cambridge University Press.

PAPAFRAGOU A, 2010. Source-goal asymmetries in motion representation: implications for language production and comprehension[J]. Cognitive science, 34: 1064-1092.

PECK J Y, LIN J X, SUN C F, 2013. Aspectual classification of mandarin Chinese verbs: a perspective of scale structure[J]. Language and linguistics, 14(4): 663-700.

PEYRAUBE A, 2006. Motion events in Chinese: a diachronic study of directional complements[M]//HICKMANN M, ROBERT S. Space in languages: linguistic systems and cognitive categories. Amsterdam: John Benjamins Publishing Company.

PINKER S, 1989. Learnability and cognition: the acquisition of argument structure [M]. Cambridge, MA: MIT Press.

POURCEL S, 2006. Relativism in the linguistic representation and cognitive conceptualisation of motion events across verb-framed and satellite-framed languages[D]. Durham: University of Durham.

PULLEYBLANK E G, 1995. Outline of classical Chinese grammar[M]. Vancouver: University of British Columbia Press.

RAMCHAND G C, 2008. Verb meaning and the lexicon: a first phase syntax[M].

Cambridge: Cambridge University Press.

RAPOPORT T, 2012. Abandoning manner-result complementarity. Around the verb workshop[D]. Paris: Sorbonne Nouvelle.

RAPPAPORT H M, 2008. Lexicalized meaning and the internal structure of events [M]//ROTHSTEIN S. Theoretical and crosslinguistic approaches to the semantics of aspect. Amsterdam: John Benjamins Publishing Company.

RAPPAPORT H M, LEVIN B, 1998. Building verb meanings[M]//BUTT M, HEUDER W. The projection of arguments: lexical and compositional factors. Stanford, CA: CSLI Publications.

RAPPAPORT H M, LEVIN B, 2010. Reflections on manner/result complementarity[M]// DORON E, RAPPAPORT HOVAV M, SICHEL I. In syntax, lexical semantics, and event structure. Oxford: Oxford University Press.

RAPPAPORT H M, LEVIN B, 2014. Building scalar changes[M]//ALEXIADOU A, BORER H, ACHÄFER F. The syntax of roots and the roots of syntax. Oxford: Oxford University Press.

SHI Y Z, 2002. The establishment of modern Chinese grammar: the formation of the resultative construction and its effects[M]. Amsterdam: John Benjamins Publishing Company.

SHI W L, WU Y C, 2014. Which way to move: the evolution of motion expressions in Chinese[J]. Linguistics, 52(5): 1237-1292.

SHI W L, WU Y C, 2015. Evolution of motion representations in Chinese: language structure, language use, and language typology[M]//SHEN J X. Zhongguo yuyanxue youxiu lunwenxuan. Berlin: De Gruyter Mouton.

SLOBIN D I, 2004. The many ways to search for a frog: linguistic typology and the expression of motion events[M]//STRÖMQVIST S, VERHOEVEN L. Relating events in narrative 2: typological and contextual perspectives. Mahwah, NJ: Lawrence Erlbaum.

SLOBIN D I, 2006. What makes manner of motion salient? Explorations in linguistic typology, discourse, and cognition[M]//HICKMANN M, ROBERT S. Space in languages: linguistic systems and cognitive categories. Amsterdam: John Benjamins Publishing Company.

STOWELL T A, 1981. Origins of phrase structure[M]. Cambridge, MA: MIT Press.

SUN C F, 1996. Word-order change and grammaticalization in the history of Chinese [M]. Redwood City. CA: Stanford University Press.

SUN C F, 2013. Chinese resultative verb compounds: lexicalization and grammaticalization [M]//CAO G S, CHAPPELL H, DJAMOURI R, et al. Breaking down the barriers: interdisciplinary studies in Chinese linguistics and beyond. Taipei: Academia Sinica.

SUN Y W, 1997. Word formation through tone alternation in classical Chinese [D]. Beijing: Peking University.

TAI J H-Y, 1984. Verbs and times in Chinese: Vendler's four categories[R]//TESTEN D, MISHRA V, DROGO J. Papers from the para session on lexical semantics. Chicago, Illinois: Chicago Linguistic Society.

TAI J H-Y, 2003. Cognitive relativism: resultative construction in Chinese[J]. Language and linguistics, 4(2): 301-316.

TALMY L, 1985. Lexicalization patterns: semantic structure in lexical forms[M]// SHOPEN T. Language typology and syntactic description 3: grammatical categories and the lexicon. Cambridge: Cambridge University Press.

TALMY L, 2000. Toward a cognitive semantics, volume II: typology and process in concept structuring[M]. Cambridge, MA: MIT Press.

TALMY L, 2009. Main verb properties and equipollent framing[M]//GUO J S, LIEVEN E, BUDWIG N, et al. Cross-linguistic approaches to the psychology of language: research in the tradition of Dan Isaac Slobin. New York: Psychology Press.

USUKI T, 2011. When Talmy's typology meets peculiar mimetics in Japanese[R]. Paper Presented in the 4th Conference of International Spring Forum.

VERKERK A, 2014. The correlation between motion event encoding and path verb lexicon size in the Indo-European language family[J]. Folia linguistica historica, 35: 307-358.

WANG L, 1980. An outline of Chinese language history[M]. Beijing: Zhonghua Book Company.

WANG Y T, 2013. A study of phonetic changes of translational verbs in ancient

Chinese: the types, conditions, rules and causes[J]. Studies in language and linguistics, 33(3): 73-86.

XIAO R, MCENERY T, 2004. Aspect in mandarin Chinese: a corpus-based study [M]. Amsterdam: John Benjamins Publishing Company.

XU D, 2013. Space in languages of China: cross-linguistic, synchronic and diachronic perspectives[M]. Beijing: World Publishing Corporation.

YANG R X, 2005. The function of semantic feature ananlysis in the research of historical syntax: evolution from "V1+V2+O" to "V+C+O" revisited[J]. Journal of Peking Univeristy, 42(2): 51-59.

YU N, 1995. Towards a definition of unaccusative verbs in Chinese[C]// CAMACHO J, CHOUEIRI L. Proceedings of the 6th North American Conference on Chinese Linguistics. Los Angeles: University of South California.

YUAN B P, 1999. Acquiring the unaccusative/unergative distinction in a second language: evidence from English-speaking learners of L2 Chinese[J]. Linguistics, 37: 275-296.

ZENG C L, 2013. "V+zou" he "V+qu". ["V+zou" and "V+qu"] [J]. Chinese teaching in the world, 1: 51-64.

ZHANG Y S, 2005. A study of word collocation evolution: case studies on some verbs and nouns before the Sui Dynasty[M]. Jinan: Shandong Qilu Press.

ZHAO Y, 2005. Causativity in L2 Chinese grammar[M]. Beijing: Peking University Press.

ZLATEV J, YANGKLANG P, 2004. A third way to travel: the place of Thai in motion-event typology[M]//STRÖMQVIST S, VERHOEVEN L. Relating events in narrative: typological and contextual perspectives. Hillsdale, NJ: Lawrence Erlbaum.